The BENNIGAN'S Guide

IRISH AMERICAN

BENNIGAN'S

GRILL & TAVERN ®

BENNIGAN'S®
GUIDE TO
BEER TASTING TIPS,
TOASTS
& FOOD

BY

ROB HAIBER

The Info Devels Inc
The Info Devel Press
La Grangeville, New York 12540
Tele: 914.223.3269
Fax: 914.227.5520
Internet: rob1bbc@earthlink.net

Copyright 1997 by S&A Restaurant Corp.
Copyright nr: 96–095430

Written by: Rob Haiber
Book design: Rob Haiber
Book cover design: The Beaird Agency
Co-editors: Peggy Marshall-Mims and W. P. Haiber

To order copies of this book, telephone: 972.404.5382 or write to:
Bennigan's Guide to Beer Tasting Tips, Toast & Food
12404 Park Central Drive
Dallas, TX 75251

First edition
ISBN: 0-944089-27-5

Printed in the United States of America by Guest Custom Printing, Woodland Hills, CA.

96 97 98 99 00
10 9 8 7 6 5 4 3 2 1
Library of Congress Cataloging-in-Publication Data
Haiber, Robert E.
Beer, beer history, beer styles. beer and food, Bennigan's restaurant directory

Although all reasonable care has been taken in the preparation of this book, neither the publisher nor the author can accept any liability for any consequences arising from the use thereof, or for the information contained herein.

DEDICATION

Dedicated to the unknown who brewed the first beer.

From thee, everything flows.

Contents

Foreword   ix

Acknowledgments   x

Introduction   xi

Chapter 1: Quest for beer knowledge   **13**
     Overview of beer
     Style color charts
     FAQs (frequently asked questions)

Chapter 2: Beer tasting tips   **27**
     How to identify, distinguish and define beer tastes
     Evaluating beer
     Beer tasting tips
     Ale & lager style profile charts
     Tasteline chart
     Sample evaluation & sequences

Chapter 3: Beer tasters' toasts   **53**

Chapter 4: Great food and beer tips   **69**

     Guidelines for beer and food combinations
     Bennigan's menu & complementary beers

Chapter 5: Copper Clover International Beer Quest®   **77**
     What is it? How to sign up?
     Tap Time™ and True Pint™
     CCIBQ restaurant locations

Chapter 6: Beer style guide   **97**

     Three styles that changed the brewing industry
     Beer style guide

Acknowledgments

Nothing is produced in a vacuum. This book would not have been produced without the help of many people.

First and foremost, I want to thank Vivian Miller, now back in her native Louisville, KY. She was there when I needed her, and kept me going mentally through the long gestation period of this book.

Matthias and Nicole Fräbel of Fielderstat, Germany, who have helped me, over the years, gather information on German brewing activities.

I would be remiss if I did not mention others, friends and colleagues, who share my interest in beer styles, and the researching of them: John Calen, with whom I have judged hundreds of beers; Alan Eames, Fred Eckhardt; Graham Lees, who has done much great work researching and writing about the beers of Munich and Bavaria; Jim Lambic Leff; Michael Jackson; Roger Protz, editor of *What's Brewing;* Dr Keith Thomas, of the University of Sunderland, with whom I have spent numerous hours discussing our findings; and Tim Webb, who's done outstanding work researching and writing about the beers of Belgium and the Netherlands.

Then there is Daniel Bradford, publisher of All About Beer Magazine, who strongly urged me (late one beery night at my local) to decide whether I wanted to be a full-time writer, or an Apple Mac consultant.

The team at The Beaird Agency – Russel CeBallos, Michelle Dubois, Yvette Hunt and Chris Sizemore, who helped immensely in creating the artwork.

Finally, a special thank you to Peggy Marshall-Mims, vice president of corporate communications at Metromedia Restaurant Group, who put in so many late hours bringing this project first to fruition, and then to completion. It was a pleasure working with her.

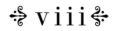

Foreword

Bennigan's celebrates the growing appreciation of specialty beers with its Copper Clover International Beer Quest, an exploration of beers from around the world. This book is designed as a beer adventure companion to help you distinguish your beer taste experiences, enhance your social occasions with a new toast, or one borrowed from history... and confidently combine beer with food selections.

As you explore beer tastes, Bennigan's encourages you to always "Think Responsibly, Drink Responsibly". You'll find this message prominently displayed throughout our restaurants. It is a visible reminder of our commitment to responsible alcohol beverage service, and it is our way of saying we care about you.

Introduction
In praise of Ale

Ale is rightly called Nappy, *for it will set a nap upon a mans threed bare eyes when he is sleepy. It is called* Merry-goe-downe *for it slides down merrily; It is fragrant to the sent; It is most pleasing to the taste; The flowering and mantling of it (like Chequer worke) with the Verdant smiling of it, is delightful to the sight; it is* Touching *or* Feeling *to the* Braine *and* Heart; *and (to please the senses all) it provokes men to singing and mirth, which is contenting to the Hearing.*

The speedy taking of it doth comfort a heavy and troubled minde; it will make a weeping widow laugh and forget sorrow for her deceased husband… It will set a Bashful suitor a-woing; It heates the chill blood of the Aged; It will cause a man to speake past his owne, or any other man's capacity, or understanding; It sets an edge upon Logick and Rhetorick; It is a friend to the Muses… *It mounts the Musitian 'bove* Eccla; *It makes the Balladmaker Rime beyond Reason, It is a Repairer of a decaied Color in the face; It puts Eloquence into the Oratour; It will make the Philospher talke profoundly, the Scholler learnedly, and the Lawyer Acute and feelingly.* Ale *at Whitsontide, or a Whitson Church* Ale, *is a repairer of decayed Countrey Churches; It is a great friend to Truth, for they that drinke of it (to the purpose) will reveale all they know, be it never so secret to be kept; It is an Embleme of Justice, for it allowes and yeelds measure; It will put Courage into a Coward and make him swagger and fight; It is a seale to many a good Bargaine. The Physitian will commend it; the Lawyer will defend it, It neither hurts, nor kils, any but those that abuse it unmeasurably and beyond bearing; It doth good to as many as take it rightly; It is as good as a paire of Spectacles to cleare the Eyesight of an old parish Clarke; And in Conclusion, it is such a nourisher of Mankinde, that if my mouth were as bigge as Bishopsgate, my Pen as long as a Maypole, and my Inke a flowing spring, or a standing fishpond, yet I could not with Mouth, Pen, or Inke, speak or write the true worth and worthinesse of* Ale.

—John Taylor (1580–1653), Drinke and Welcome
John Taylor is the earliest known English language author who made his livelihood writing about beer. He is considered the father of all beer writers.

Chapter 1

Embarking on a Quest for higher knowledge about beer

WELCOME TO A new world of beer tastes. It's part of a consumer trend Bennigan's identifies as a *taste sensation celebration*, encompassing both food and beverages. Just as we have become more adventuresome with unique, bold tastes for foods we prefer, so too, are we exploring beer with new-found interest. Discovering diverse beer flavor profiles offers opportunities to savor exciting beer and food taste sensations.

This taste adventure trend, along with the renaissance of specialty beers, has spurred enthusiastic curiosity about beer. There's plenty there to explore. Beer is a pretty heady subject, beyond the foam on top of our pints, mugs, and pilsner glasses. Beer is ingrained in our culture, and reflective of lifestyles throughout history, from ancient Mesopotamia to the present.

As you embark on your quest for higher knowledge about beer, this book can serve as your traveler's guide. First, it will provide you with a quick-study background on the basics about beer. Building on this foundation of knowledge, it will guide you through an easy process to identify and evaluate beers, provide helpful tools to help you experiment with beer and food tastes, and offer toasts to enhance your social occasions. So, welcome to the beer taste revolution! A time some have called the age of drinking less, but better and smarter. Now, on with the Quest!

What is beer?

B EER IS A GENERIC term for alcohol beverages made by fermenting barley, a cereal grain (or mixture of several others such as wheat, oats, rye), and flavored with hops. It is important to note that hops must be used for a grain-fermented beverage to be considered beer. For example, malt whiskey begins as a malt-fermented beverage, but hops are not used in it.

Sometimes called liquid bread, beer and bread have the same ingredients—water, grain, and yeast. Beer also has many of the same nutrients—carbohydrates, calcium, thiamin, riboflavin, and niacin.

Beer was one of the earliest beverages, with evidence of the first brews dating back 8,000 years to Mesopotamia (modern Iraq). In the early days, and throughout much of beer's history, it was the preferred daily beverage because surface water supplies were not safe, a condition that did not change until the 20th century.

Crossing the rough north Atlantic, beer played a role in the settling of America. With shipboard beer supplies nearly exhausted, the Mayflower Pilgrims (1620), changed plans to sail further south to the Virginia colony, and warmer climates. Instead, they landed at

Plymouth Rock. Beer was the beverage of choice during the colonial period, and has remained so ever since.

Throughout the years, beer played a role in the development of our culture. The centerpiece of our neighborhood communities was the local tavern, where beers were shared, friendships formed, and customs were celebrated. Special beers were brewed for all sorts of occasions. As just one example, the word bridal comes from Bride-ale. The custom, in Old England and Colonial America was that before her wedding day, a woman brewed a special ale. She then sold it on her wedding day to finance the start of the new household.

How is beer made?

BREWING BEER IS BOTH an art and a science. At its highest level, brewing is a very technical process. For the purposes of this discussion, we'll avoid brewerspeak, and cover the basics.

Gristing & mashing

Malted barley (and whatever other grains are called for, as per style) is first crushed in a grist mill, and then added to hot (65–67°C, 149–153°F) water, in a vessel called a mash- or lauter tun. This stage is called mashing. Here the malted grains are steeped, much as is tea. During mashing, the carbohydrates contained in malt are converted to fermentable sugars, which the yeast will then digest and turn into alcohol and other substances.

The Boil

When mashing is complete, after about 90 minutes, the hot liquid, now called wort (pronounced wurt), is pumped into another tun called a brew kettle or copper (after the metal of which they are often constructed).

The wort is then brought to a boil, at which point hops are added. Boils typically last 90 minutes. There are five main reasons for the boil. First, to destroy any enzymes that might have survived the mash. Second, to destroy any micro-organisms in both the wort and the hops. Third, to extract bitterness from the hops. Fourth, to concentrate the wort. Fifth, to clarify the wort by coagulating polyphenols and proteins, which drop out of suspension. The last two items involve complex chemical processes beyond the scope of this discussion.

When the boil is complete, the hot wort is often left to stand. Some aromatic hops may be added then, or typically 5 minutes before the end of the boil. The hops then settle to the bottom of the copper and make a bed. The hot wort is then drained through the hop bed, which acts as a filter for suspended particles in the wort. It is run through a heat exchanger, to lower the temperature, and into the primary ferment tank, or fermenter.

Aeration & fermentation

Fermentation is the next stage, and may take place in open-fermenters or enclosed vessels, depending on brewery practice.

When the wort temperature drops below, say, 75°F, the yeast is added. The act is called pitching. What is important to note is that each and every yeast strain has an optimal temperature at which it works best. Ferment temperatures other than the optimal may provoke the yeast into producing off-flavors and odors.

Air is introduced into the now-cooled wort in a process called aeration. This is necessary because the yeast need to first multiply, which they do until all the oxygen is consumed. They then switch to anaerobic respiration, and begin to digest the malt sugars in the wort. The latter process normally takes three to seven days, during which the yeast produce about even parts of alcohol and carbon dioxide. The yeast also produce huge heads of creamy foam. Some brewers skim this yeast-laden foam. Others let it settle out.

Racking & Conditioning

The now-young, or green, beer is now removed from the primary fermenter, a process called racking. At this stage, the young beer may be racked directly to casks, in the English tradition, and conditioned in them. Otherwise the beer is racked into secondary ferment tanks for additional, end-phase fermentation, conditioning, and clarification, as suspended yeast and other particles (called colloidals) settle out.

After secondary conditioning, which lasts for 10–14 days for ales, and up to several months for lagers, the beer is ready to be either bottled, canned, or kegged. In most cases, the beer is pumped from the secondary fermenting vessels through a filter, which removes yeast and colloidals.

Note that bottle-conditioned beer, that is beer that is bottled with its own yeast, is not filtered. The beer is slightly primed with additional sugars, which the yeast digest. That process produces enough carbondioxide, which is absorbed into the beer in the bottle, that the beer is properly conditioned, or fizzy.

Overview of beer styles

There are just two classifications of beer–ale and lager. Within each classification, there are many different styles of beer, ranging from ultra-pale to the blackest of stouts. The determining factor that scientifically places a particular beer in one category or the other is the yeast type used. While there are many strains of yeast, (some suitable for brewing and others that are not), they are divided into top-fermenting and bottom-fermenting types. To keep which is which straight in mind, think of top as above, and bottom as lower. The first letter of Above and Ale match; the first letter of Lower and Lager match.

Another distinguishing characteristic between ale and lager yeast is the temperature at which they are active. Ale yeasts ferment best at temperatures of 15–25°C (59–77°F). Lager yeast works best at 3–11°C (38–52°F), but can work down to as low as 1°C (34°F). It is easy to guess what type beer is in the barrels, when one examines photographs of cold-looking beer storage cellars and caverns.

There are also some beer hybrid styles, which interchange yeasts and their normal fermentation temperatures. Two of these are genuinely American, and developed in the late 19th century.

A comprehensive style guide, Chapter 6, is meant to give you a sense of the scope of the styles brewers produce as well as a little more detailed history on some of the styles. Some styles are extremely old, dating almost to man's earliest attempts at brewing. Others are relatively new. Still others are making a comeback, after being abandoned by brewers for decades (or longer).

The charts that follow will give you an overview of most of the beer styles, as they are grouped by color, and then by ale, lager, and hybrid categories.

Light-colored beer styles

Ale	Lager	Hybrids
Golden Mild	NABLAB*	Cream Ale
Golden Pale Ale	Dry	Malt Liquor
Golden Strong	Ice	Sparkling Lager Ale
Berliner Weisse	Economy	Kölsch
Weizen	Standard	
Witbier	Premium	
Helles Weizenbock	Craft	
Tripel	Pilsner	
Lambic	European	
	Tropical	
	Export	
	Helles	
	Helles Bock	
	Diät Pilsner	
	Maibock	

* Non-Alcohol Beers / Low Alcohol Beers

Amber-colored beer styles

Ale	Lager	Hybrid
Alt	Bière de Paris	
Best Bitter	Märzen	
Bière de garde	Oktoberfest	
Bitter	Vienna	
ESB		
Gueuze		
IPA		
Irish		
Pale Ale		
Scottish		
Welsh		

Dark-colored beer styles

Ale	Lager	Hybrid
Barleywine	Bockbier	Porter Lager
Browns	Doppelbock	
Dunkelweizen	Euro Dark	
Grätzer	Rauchbier	
Mild	Schwarzbier	
Old		
Porters		
Scotch		
Stouts		

Frequently asked questions

THE RESURGENT INTEREST in beer has provoked all manner of questions about it. So, to borrow from the computer industry and internet publishers, here is a list of some frequently asked questions.

What's the difference between ale and lager?

The simple difference can be put down to the scientific classification of the yeast, a single-celled organism, used in making a particular brand. Ale yeast, or top-fermenting yeast, performs its magic at the upper reaches of a ferment tank. This type yeast does its work (fermenting malt) best at 15–25°C (59–77°F). Lager yeast, or bottom-fermenting yeast, works towards the bottom of the ferment tank, and works best at 3–11°C (38–52°F). To keep which is which clearly in mind, think ale-above; lager-lower. Of the two, lager yeast is a relatively new class. It was developed in the early 1800s, whereas ale yeast has been in existence since creation.

I've seen some beer bottles with sediment at the bottom. Are those bad bottles which should be avoided?

Several years ago the answer might very well have been yes–that what you saw was, in fact, residue from improperly filtered beer. Today, probably not. What you observed is yeast that has settled out of suspension in bottle-conditioned beers. Rather than filtering yeast from the beer before bottling, then charging the bottle with carbon dioxide, more brewers are leaving the yeast in the beer, where it produces its own natural carbonation, held by experts to be superior in quality. This practice is most common with British and Belgian ale, and German wheat beer. It is now gaining acceptance with some North American craft brewers, too.

What are hops and malt?

Both spring from the good earth. The hop plant, of which there are many varieties, is a climbing vine, which may grow to over 20 feet high, in temperate climates. The cones of the plant are used as the prime bittering agent in beer. Without it, beer would be sickeningly sweet.

Malt is a man-made derivative of grain. In brewing, malted barley is used, though sometimes wheat, rye or other cereals are used with it. To yeast, malt is food. As a by-product of digestion, yeast produces alcohol, carbon dioxide, and many other chemical compounds.

Correctly used, as in any recipe, hops and malt make the beverage we call beer.

What's the best beer?

This is the question which makes every beer judge cringe. With nearly 100 beer styles and sub-styles, and tens of thousands of brands extant, how can one properly answer? It's impossible.

Yes, there are some brands that are considered by many experts to be world-class. There are contrary experts who disagree. Who's right? Who's wrong? With such a subjective matter as personal taste, beauty is in the eye of the beholder, or, in this case, the beer taster. To loosely translate the Italian expression, *Tutti i gusti, sono gusti,* to each his own.

Bill Woodring, a colleague, answers best: "The beer in my hand".

Why are there several different ways the alcohol content of beer is measured and indicated?

Just as temperature is measured by several different scientific scales: Celsius, Fahrenheit or Kelvin, so too is beer's alcohol content. There are three scales that are rather obscure, used mostly by brewers. They are Balling, Plato, and Brix. Balling was developed in 1843 by Carl Joseph Napolean Balling. Around 1900 it was discovered that Balling's tables were slightly erroneous, and were corrected with new tables called Plato, after Dr. Plato, a German. The Brix scale is a variation of Plato, but calibrated at 15°C (59°F) instead of 17.5°C (64°F) used in the Plato scale.

There are three more common scales in use today. They are alcohol by weight (ABW), by volume (ABV), and 'brewer's degrees' called "original gravity" and designated OG. ABW is used in Germany and the United States by some large brewers. It is rather confusing, as very few people know to reckon liquid by weight. ABV is used in Canada and Great Britain, and by most craft brewers in North America. If a beer is labelled 5.0% ABV, it is much easier to look at its container and see 5.0% of its volume than to reckon 3.98% of its weight. The use of OG is becoming practice in North America, too. It is used by both craft-brewers and home-brewers, with whom it really took root. This British brewers' scale is very easy to use. Brewers always measure the original gravity of wort before they ferment it. This measurement tells them how much fermentable sugars are in the wort, thereby indicating what the alcohol content will be. If a brewer gets an OG reading of 1050 (technically it is 1.050, but brewers often drop the decimal point, and say it "ten-fifty"), he is pretty much assured that the ABV will be 5.0%. In British pubs, by law, the alcohol content of every beer dispensed must be clearly indicated. This is most often done with pump-clips on the dispense mechanism. These pump-clips show the name of the beer, the brewery, and, most often the OG, though some indicate ABV.

The British system is designed as much for consumer protection, as for caution. No one can claim in court they didn't know how strong the beers they drank were. Too, beer drinkers there (often called 'punters') know more about the beers they are buying.

Dark beers have more alcohol, don't they?

In a word, no. Beer color has no bearing on alcohol strength. To clearly illustrate this: the English have a session (low alcohol) beer called Mild that is usually dark brown. Compare Mild with Dubuisson, the Belgian brewer's, blonde Bush Beer (Scaldis in the States). Typically, Mild is brewed at 3.0–4.0% ABV. Bush Beer weighs in at a massive 12.0% ABV. That said, darker colored beers tend to be more flavorful than lighter colored ones.

At what temperature should beer be served?

That depends on if the beer in question is an ale or a lager. Ales are at their most delicious when served at about 13–16°C (55–60°F). Some ale styles even improve as they warm above that temperature. The optimal serving temperature for lagers is 6–9°C (42–48°F). The tradition in America has been to drink beer at much colder temperatures. With more people now seeking knowledge about beer, we may someday see a shift in temperature preferences to more closely align with the ideal temperature for best tastes. And perhaps someday the thought of drinking ice cold beer would seem as taboo as drinking ice cold burgundy wine or warm chablis.

Is clear, green, or brown the best color for beer bottles?

Clear glass admits light, which is bad news for beer because it causes a chemical reaction in the beer that is the source of skunky odors. Beer judges refer to such beer as being lightstruck. Green glass is no better than clear. Brown is best because it blocks light from passing through the bottle.

How long will bottled beer keep before it goes bad?

That depends on many factors. Along with light, heat is an enemy of beer. The warmer it is stored once it it leaves the brewery, the shorter its shelf-life will be. Alcohol content also plays a huge role. The stronger the beer, the longer it will last. For example, Eldridge Pope's Thomas Hardy Ale, at 12% ABV is recorded to last up to 25 years. Samuel Adams Triple Bock, at a massive 17±% ABV, should last that long, too. Most modern craft brewers use a 90–120-day period from the bottling date. This does not mean that at the stroke of midnight on the sell-by date the beer automatically turns bad. Stick to beers that have clearly indicated, plain-English "sell by" dates on their labels.

Chapter 2

Defining beer tastes
Evaluating beer

THE FUN OF EXPLORING beer styles begins with discovering the diverse ranges of tastes–from the crisp, fresh, floral bitterness of a Pilsner Urquell, to the molasses-apple flavor of a Paulaner Salvator Doppelbock in the lager category. As for ales, you can travel the taste trails from the musty, smoky bitterness of Sierra Nevada Pale Ale, to the sweet fruitiness and soft fizziness of Timmerman's Peche Lambic. The landscape of beer tastes is filled with all kinds of terrain, providing a thrilling ride for your taste buds. The more you venture out, the more keen sense of taste you'll develop, allowing you to easily recognize the more subtle characteristics of beer styles.

As you explore, you'll also acquire knowledge about beer styles and history, providing excellent fodder for social events. Just imagine, you're sitting next to your boss at a company dinner, and he orders a Dos Equis along with fajitas. Think about what an impression you'll make with this bit of trivia:

Did you know that the Vienna Lagers brewed in Mexico are actually the only true examples still being brewed? In fact, at the turn of the 19th century, this style was probably the most popular style of beer in Austria. When the style was no longer vogue in Vienna, it turned up in Mexico, brought there by immigrant Austrian brewers, and today the Mexican versions remain the only representatives of this beer style.

You're sure to score some extra points with your boss for your knowledge of international beer history.

So what tools do you need to learn how to distinguish beer flavors? In addition to your senses–sight, smell, taste and touch–you need a working beer language for discussion and debate. You also need an understanding of beer styles, with a uniform evaluation process to put your flavor experiences in context.

Let's begin with a glossary of flavor terminology. I've kept it simple to avoid as much jargon as possible.

General terms

Beer flavor: flavor is a combination of aroma and tastes, which may be influenced by temperature and tactile sensations.

Nose: the odor, perfume or scent of a beer.

Notes: a descriptive term for the aromas and tastes in a beer, with an indication of where they are sensed. For example, if you sense soft maltiness in the taste, it can be described as, "Lovely malt notes on the palate".

Palate: sense of taste; mental taste; loosely used to describe where one senses flavor, when describing a beer.

Finish: the tastes in the mouth commencing shortly after one has swallowed a mouthful of beer. The finish of beers runs the gamut from practically non-existent to very long after-taste. A brief finish might hardly be noticeable at all, while a long one may linger in the mouth, slowly diminishing over a half-hour or more.

There are actually three distinct phases of the finish: the initial, the middle, and the end, as the tongue and palate react to the beer.

As a rule of thumb, the more characterful and flavorful the beer, the longer its finish.

Quality of finish: this relates to how good (or bad) the finish actually is, not its duration. The quality of a finish may be delightful, pleasant, boring, interesting, harsh, unpleasant. Numerous words may be used to describe its quality. It is an individual matter.

Taste descriptions

Each of us interprets sensations differently, so taste descriptions and evaluations will vary. There are no wrong taste evaluations. These descriptions are provided as a guide, and perhaps they will inspire new taste profile definitions.

Acidic or sour: lactic or citric sourness or acidity is associated with some beer styles, and is often present to a minimal degree in others. It is sensed by a puckering and certain dryness in the mouth, especially on the inner cheeks. A similar sensation may be experienced by eating a lemon or a grapefruit. Acidity is sensed along the sides of the tongue.

Acetic: vinegary. May also be detected in the nose.

Bitter: a taste induced by hops and, often, by other compounds in beer. Bitterness may be pleasant or, if overdone, unpleasant. Bitterness is the counterbalance to malt sweetness, and is sensed at the very back of the tongue.

Complex: having many sensations on the palate.

Crisp: very lively carbonation.

Oversweet: cloying sweetness, or sickeningly sweet flavor, that leaves the palate feeling coated. High levels of sweetness may also be detected in the odor.

Robust: hearty; rich; lingering.

Salty: salty tastes may be present in a beer. Saltiness is sensed on both sides of the tongue, just back from the tip of it.

Sweet: sweet may be either good or bad, depending on the amount of sweetness, and its appropriateness to the style of beer in which it is found. Sweetness comes from the malt, and is sensed at the tip of the tongue.

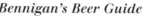

Timid: flavor dissipates quickly.

Other self-explanatory descriptions: buttery, caramel, chocolate, fruity, nutty, roasty, spicy.

Body descriptions

These refer to the viscosity of the beer. The maltier and stronger the beer, the heavier its body. I can think of no quicker way to learn body than to compare the body of a Pilsner with that of a Barleywine, or an Imperial Stout. This is one of the trickiest bits to learn and get right.

Full-bodied: the beer feels somewhat thick in the mouth.

Medium-bodied: a very wide range between the two extremes. Most beers are medium-bodied.

Thin-bodied: close to water; what most beer styles should not be like. The thinner the body, the less character a beer will have.

Mouthfeel descriptions

These refer to the specific sensations a beer triggers by physical contact with the inside the mouth and tongue. One particularly sensitive area is the inner lips, where a tingling sensation is often felt, when stimulated by higher alcohols compounds or phenols.

Alkaline: dryness and a puckering sensation of the inner cheeks.

Astringent: can best be described as mouth-puckering, tart, or tannin-like sensations.

Carbonation: this is apparent in the amount of fizziness in a beer. Beer styles have developed differing carbonation rates over the years. Pilsners, some North American lager, and wheat beer are highly carbonated. British ales, however, are not. The sensation is felt as a tingling on the tongue, and briefly on the inner cheeks.

Dry: lacking sweetness, but not to be confused with tartness.

Metallic: the taste of coins, iron, or rusty water in the palate.

Powdery: these sensations might have a mouthfeel that is chalky, silicous, or like dusty cushions.

Warming: is induced by high levels of alcohol. One should begin to sense this when the alcohol content exceeds, say, 5.5–6.0% ABV (Alcohol By Volume), as found in Barleywine, Bocks, and Old Ale.

Evaluating beer

THERE ARE MANY ways to evaluate beer, ranging from the hedonistic (judging from pleasure-criteria alone) to those used by beer judges. For the purposes of this book, it will be kept simple: a straightforward judgement of criteria in nine steps.

1. appearance
2. foam/head
3. aroma/odor
4. body
5. aroma/bouquet
6. carbonation rate
7. hops/malt balance
8. quality of finish
9. overall impressions

The first eight items are all based on what is appropriate for the style of beer one is drinking. The last is a subjective appraisal. To check beer style characteristics, see the charts in this section, or the detailed style guide in Chapter 6. Some steps overlap, or are done concurrently. It is important to examine each in turn. One takes a sip to evaluate body, say, but one simultaneously senses the carbonation and hop/malt balance, and soon, the finish. Yet one must concentrate on evaluating the body and not the others.

For those of you who might be interested in starting your own log-books, I've taken the liberty to include the points judges award each item beside the item heading. They add up to 50 points in all. All commercial beers should score 30 points or more.

On page 35, you'll find the Bennigan's Beer Evaluation Scorecard™ developed to help guests learn and evaluate beer. The scorecard uses the nine criteria discussed in this book.

Since each of us perceives sensations differently, there are no absolutes, only unto each person. In the end, we each determine for ourselves whether we like a beer or not. The Bennigan's Beer Evaluation Scorecard has a special section for your Personal Taste Profile Ratings, using a 5-pint rating system similar to the 5-star rating for restaurants.

At the end of this section, you'll find some helpful tips to use when evaluating beer. These tips are on page 38.

Now, on to the details for each of the nine evaluation steps Beneath each are point options to be assigned, depending on what you find. The criteria and assigned points are adapted from a German professional beer judges' form I modified to better suit beer evaluation as it's done in North America.

Step 1: appearance (5pt)

Check for clarity. Hold the glass up to a light source. Are there any unidentifiable objects floating in it? Sometimes debris results from clotted yeast. If not, the beer passes. Be careful not to pour out the yeast sediment in bottle-conditioned beer. A drop or two will cloud a glass of beer. An exception is German-style wheat beers where it is the custom to pour out and drink the yeast with the beer. Yeast has many healthful nutrients. In this case, cloudiness is normal and expected.

> **Point options:**
> (5) Color to type; totally clear, or evenly cloudy, eg hefe Weissebier
> (4) Color still to type; clear, or cloudy, but evenly dispersed
> (3) Color not to type; moderately cloudy, or unevenly dispersed yeast
> (2) Color faulty; cloudy or clumpy yeast
> (1) Color very much not to type; very cloudy, or very clumpy yeast

Note: The points scale would be reversed, if having a beer meant to be drunk with its yeast, as noted above.

Step 2: foam/head (5pt)

Examine the head. Is it big and creamy? Is it absent? Or is it somewhere in between? Wheat beers toss huge heads. Very strong ales, such as Barleywine, that are bottle-conditioned (beer aged in the bottle with yeast) are almost always flat. The other styles range between the extremes. If a beer that should normally have a decent head lacks one, it is a warning that problems exist, which will show up in one or more of the following criteria.

Foam lacing down the inside of the glass is lovely, but indicative of nothing much, except, perhaps, a very clean glass. The higher the alcohol content, the less lacing there will be.

Point options:
(5) Head good and lasting
(4) Head still good, moderate duration
(3) Head deficient, fairly short duration
(2) Head faulty, very short duration
(1) Bad head; immediately disintegrates

Note: the point scale would be reversed if drinking a style that does not throw a big head, such as a Barleywine.

Step 3: aroma/odor (5pt)

Here one is looking for either a clean odor, or for defects, not associated with ingredients, but with the brewing process, such as infections from bacteria or wild yeast. The most common off-odors, from among hundreds are skunkiness from being lightstruck; wet paper, or cardboard smells associated with oxidation, buttery or butterscotch notes linked with incorrect ferment temperatures; sulphur odors from wild yeast contamination, sour-lactic notes from lactobacillus contamination, and solvent-like odors from too-warm fermentation temperatures.

Point options:
(5) Clean
(4) Nearly clean

(3) Slightly unclean
(2) Distinctly foul-smelling
(1) Strongly foul-smelling

Step 4: body (5pt)

Depending on the style, the body of beer runs the gamut from thin (watery) to full (thick). As alcohol content recedes from 5.0% ABV, the thinner a beer will be. Because less malt was used in the brewing process, the less there will be at the end to increase body. As it is, beer is nearly all water to begin with. Too, the less barley malt used, and the more rice and corn used to make the beer, the thinner it will be.

Point options:
(5) Full-bodied (to type)
(4) Approximately full-bodied
(3) Slightly full-bodied
(2) It leaves much to be desired
(1) Watery, thick of corn, thick, muddy or syrupy

Note: this is another area where the style dictates how to award points. The points awarded might reverse depending on which style beer is being evaluated. For instance, a Light Lager would get five points for being thin, not the single point indicated here. Scotch Ale, a full bodied beer should receive five points for being full-bodied.

Step 5: aroma/bouquet (5pt)

This is also called "nose". As a rule, the darker a beer is, the more character there is in the nose. Pilsners, for example are most often characterized as having floral, hoppy notes in the nose, with perhaps some underlying soft maltiness. Once the color reaches copper, then other scents begin to appear: vanilla, orange marmalade, ripe fruit, molasses, licorice, biscuits, coffee, toast, leather, toffee, different nuts, pepper and other spices, horse blanket, wet diapers, earth, port, sherry, vinous, etc. These scents can be attributed to the types of grains used and, most importantly, the strain of yeast used. Each strain imparts its own scents to the beer as a result of its digestion of malt. Most brewers carefully choose which strain they will employ to attain their desired results. There is no right or wrong with any aroma you might detect. People who regularly prepare food are often very good at identifying aromas in beer.

BEER EVALUATION SCORECARD™

EMBARK ON A QUEST FOR HIGHER KNOWLEDGE ABOUT BEER

think responsibly.
drink responsibly.

BRAND:_____ **BEER STYLE:**_____

Circle the point score for each criteria in all 9 steps. Total all points below.

Most Points | | STEP 1: APPEARANCE | | **Least Points**

5	4	3	2	1
Color & clarity to style				Off style; clumpy

STEP 2: FOAM / HEAD

5	4	3	2	1
Good & lasting				Instantly disintegrates

STEP 3: AROMA / ODOR

5	4	3	2	1
Clean				Strongly foul smell

STEP 4: BODY

5	4	3	2	1
Full bodied				Watery, thin

STEP 5: AROMA / BOUQUET

5	4	3	2	1
Pleasant to style				Strongly faulty

STEP 6: CARBONATION RATE

5	4	3	2	1
Pleasantly Fizzy				Very flat

STEP 7: HOP / MALT BALANCE

5	4	3	2	1
Distinctly good				Not perceptible

STEP 8: QUALITY & CHARACTER OF FINISH

5	4	3	2	1
Very fine, lingering				Very unpleasant

STEP 9: PERSONAL TASTE PROFILE RATINGS

Exceptional	**Real Winner**	**Middle of the Pack**	**Under Achiever**	**Definite Loser**
First choice brew; on top of my wish list; dream about it at night	Makes my day; recommend to others; repeat evaluations a must	OK to drink, but nothing to write home about; What's next?	Falls short of the mark; would be embarrassed to give to beer geeks	Taste profile targeted for visitors from another planet; first & last sample
10 pts.	8 pts.	6 pts.	4 pts.	2 pts.

OVERALL POINT SCORE: [   ] **(TOTAL ALL POINTS FROM STEPS 1-9)**

Point options:
(5) To type; agreeable, pleasant, very fine
(4) Approximately to type; nearly very fine
(3) Aroma not to type, neutral, or slightly
    agreeable or obtrusive
(2) Aroma faulty, unpleasant, very obtrusive
(1) Aroma strongly faulty

Step 6: carbonation rate or character (5pt)

This item is the one tactile stage of evaluating beer. Though not often considered, the fizziness of a beer in the mouth has great influence on how and what we taste. There is a certain fineness to carbonation that is not, at first, easy to learn to identify. Light-colored lagers and wheat beers, as a rule, are fizzier than other styles. As one swirls a sip of beer round one's mouth prior to swallowing, the carbon dioxide in suspension is released, most notably on the tongue. Too much can be off-putting to certain styles, but refreshingly right for others. Also, the stronger a beer is, the less fizziness is found.

Point options:
(5) Pleasantly fizzy or very nearly flat: perfect
(4) Fizzy, lively or nearly flat
(3) Slightly fizzy
(2) Flat, very few bubbles or fizzy, lively
(1) Very flat or overly lively

Note: scales may reverse, as styles dictate. For example, a Weizenbier should be very fizzy and, if so, should get five points. If it were flat, then one point. An extremely fizzy Barleywine should receive one point, and a flat one should get five points. This is why knowing the style parameters is so important.

Step 7: hops/malt balance (5pt)

You've already had a taste of the beer at the body stage of the evaluation, and made some initial impressions. Now take another sip and this time concentrate on what your tastebuds signal. Do you taste malt sweetness, but that quickly gives way to strong hop bitterness, or does the malt remain predominant throughout? Does the hop bitterness immediately attack your tastebuds, and you can't even find any malt? Each style has its own correct balance. This is not to say that there is only one correct combination of malt and hops that every brewer seeks. This would lead to all beers in a style tasting the same. Indeed, each brewer gives his own interpretation, hoping to strike a good balance that is a hallmark of an excellent example of a particular style. Beer isn't a generic one-taste beverage, but one with hundreds, if not thousands, of different characteristics. That is why we evaluate each beer we drink.

Point options:
(5) Distinctly good, perceptible
(4) Nearly very good, perceptible
(3) Something perceptible
(2) Scarcely perceptible
(1) Not perceptible

Note: Perceptible refers first to the perceived presence of hops and malt, then whether they are in balance according to style.

Step 8: quality and character of the finish (5pt)

Some believe the best beers are those whose taste and finishes immediately disappear after each sip. This is not so. The enjoyment of beer is as much associated with the finish as any other component. The finish can make or break a beer. Is it too dry or harsh for the style, or too malty? Are there any unpleasing tastes, or are there none? Does the finish pleasantly linger, or does it immediately disappear.

Sometimes flaws are very difficult to detect. These often come across as the feeling that something isn't quite right. The more one senses this, the lower the quality of the finish is. Overall, one should look for pleasantness, character, harmony, and, perhaps, sublime tastes in the finish.

Point options:
(5) Very fine
(4) Fine
(3) Something unpleasant (noticeable)
(2) Unpleasant
(1) Very unpleasant

Step 9: overall impressions (10pt)

Here is where one can break away from stylistic constraints, and give a purely subjective evaluation of the beer in hand. At its simplest, how much do you like the beer? See the Personal Taste Profile Ratings on the Bennigan's Scorecard (on page 35) for suggested guidelines.

Beer evaluation guidelines and tips

Never evaluate beer when under the weather, especially if your nose is stuffed up or under allergy attack.

Avoid smoking areas, where possible, as the strong smell of tobacco masks many of the delicate aromas and odors you are attempting to smell.

Make time to sniff different spices, herbs, and other food flavorings. Become aware of how things smell, whether they be flowers, plants, leather, blankets, dirt, plastics, household items, metals, moldy bread, other food items, and so on. Many beer styles have smells of everyday items. If you smell horse-blanket in a Bière de garde, then it is horse-blanket you smell. There is no right or wrong in naming odors you identify. Those who spend a lot of time preparing food, perhaps because they are used to using their noses when cooking, are very adept at identifying smells.

Always use a clean, well-rinsed glass. Do not dry the glass with paper towels, as wet paper is an off-odor found in stale beer. Rinse the glass after each use. Residual soap and body oils can completely suppress the head of a beer.

Taste beer at its optimal temperatures, if possible. Ideally, ales should be tasted at cellar temperatures: 13–16°C (55–60°F). Lagers should be served at 6-9°C (42-48°F). The temperature preferences in America have been lower, resulting in colder serving temperatures at most establishments. Ask for an unchilled glass or clasp your hands around the glass to warm it.

Don't fill the glass all the way to the top. Leave plenty of space (at least a half-glass) for the aromas and odors to accumulate. After you have learned to properly evaluate beer, 2–4oz is all you should need to do so.

Learn to get it in one or two sips—three sips max. Otherwise, you might consume too much. Getting drunk while evaluating beer is a sure way to get it wrong. Oh, and yes, beer tasters do swallow the beer.

Rinse your mouth with cool water between each beer you drink. Eating some unsalted bread or crackers does much to eradicate the taste of the previous beer.

Bear in mind that beer will taste different, if consumed with food. Revisit any distinctive or otherwise good beer you come across when eating. Taste it before eating foods, so you can more properly evaluate it.

When smelling a beer, do not shove your nose all the way down inside the glass. That is a sure way to overload the receptors in your nose. Once overloaded, however, it takes a short time for them to recover. Rather, place your nose about one inch above the rim of the glass. There is a sweet spot there, an invisible spillway of aroma molecules rising from the surface of the beer one can actually sense. Move the glass closer or farther from your nose till you find that spot. Once located, you can maintain that distance, and sniff away to your heart's content.

If you are evaluating a flight (more than one) of beers, always drink from the lightest-colored, blandest beer to the darkest ones, which have more (and stronger) flavors. The optimum would be to evaluate only beers of a single style, but that isn't always the case. Don't go to Bennigan's and have a Guinness Stout as your first beer, then switch to Pilsner Urquelle. The strong burnt barley and coffee notes of the Stout will overwhelm any subsequent light lager you might choose to drink.

Fruited beer should be drunk between any light-colored beers and dark ones. More attention should be paid to clearing the palate after drinking these beers.

Ale Style Profile

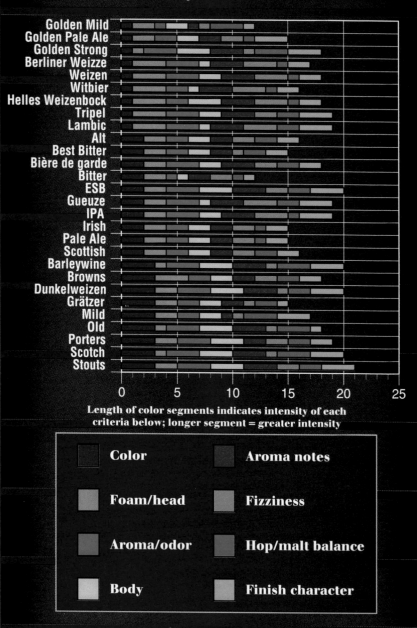

Length of color segments indicates intensity of each
criteria below; longer segment = greater intensity

Color   Aroma notes

Foam/head   Fizziness

Aroma/odor   Hop/malt balance

Body   Finish character

Sample beer evaluation

Let's step through an actual tasting of a beer, using the nine criteria previously explained, and look at it with a critical eye (nose, and palate).

Okay. It's time for me to select a beer for evaluation. We'll use this evaluation as a foundation upon which you can sample every beer you taste from now on.

My hand is on the Style Wheel... and I've just given it a forceful spin. The Wheel's spinning quite quickly now! I can't make out the style names just yet! What's it going to be?!?!? A Belgian Framboise? A Pacific Coast Pale Ale??? The Wheel's starting to slow now. I can just begin to make out some of the names! Yes! I can see Bass Ale! And there's Samuel Adams Cherry Wheat! Slowing more now... light or dark, bitter or malty... I can hardly wait! Wherever it stops, we'll have a dandy selection... The Wheel is nearly stopped now! Wow! We just missed Pete's Wicked Seasonal! And there goes Hacker-Pschorr Weisse! And it's going to be... ! ... Yes, we have a winner! It's from Ireland (how appropriate!) and it's Murphy's Irish Stout!!! Yes! What a cracker!

You have your glasses at the ready. I'll pour. Pffffst! Yes! We have a good bottle here. Carbonation sounds about right in the bottle. We'll see in just a second.

Try to ration your sample beer so you have one or two sips left at step 9. Then you'll be able to go back and reassess any previous stage you might still be contemplating. The nature of beer changes with time, and you might uncover some additional aromas or taste notes that weren't apparent earlier.

Now, let's get back to our sampling.

The pour is important. The optimum way to do it is to hold the glass several inches below the bottle, and let the beer splash right down to the bottom. This agitates the beer, which will cause it to throw a nice head. We want that. After about 2 ounces have been poured, tilt the glass so the rest of the beer sample pours down the side, then bring the glass upright.

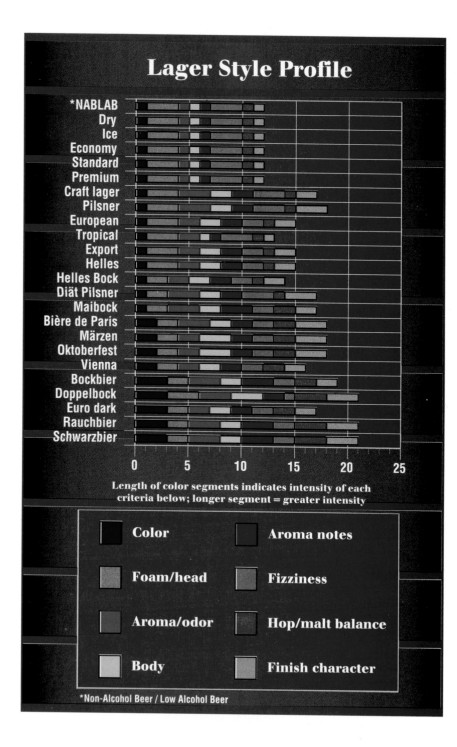

Lager Style Profile

*NABLAB
Dry
Ice
Economy
Standard
Premium
Craft lager
Pilsner
European
Tropical
Export
Helles
Helles Bock
Diät Pilsner
Maibock
Bière de Paris
Märzen
Oktoberfest
Vienna
Bockbier
Doppelbock
Euro dark
Rauchbier
Schwarzbier

0   5   10   15   20   25

Length of color segments indicates intensity of each
criteria below; longer segment = greater intensity

Color   Aroma notes

Foam/head   Fizziness

Aroma/odor   Hop/malt balance

Body   Finish character

*Non-Alcohol Beer / Low Alcohol Beer

❖ 42 ❖

Appearance – color/clarity (5pt)

The first thing to examine is the beer's color and clarity. Every beer must be assessed in relation to the style. In this case, a Stout should be dark brown to opaque black. We find Murphy's to be a very dark brown, well within the style parameters. Clarity is nearly impossible to check with a beer this dark. Even using a mini flashlight will not reveal much. Sometimes by steeply tilting the glass, holding it up to a strong light and looking at the beer just below the surface, one might be able to see some cloudiness. Murphy's is fine.

I awarded the full five points.

Foam/head (5pt)

Murphy's throws a deep tan, thick, dense, creamy head, which is appropriate for the style. Duration is fairly long, again appropriate for the style.

I awarded the full five points.

Aroma/odor (5pt)

At this step, it is time to take a first long sniff. There is a trick to this I want to share with you. The nose is a very sensitive organ. It can very easily be overwhelmed by odors. When this happens, several minutes must pass before it regains its sensitivity. If you shove your nose into a glass of beer and take a big whiff, your nose will surely lose its sensitivity. However, there is a technique I learned by chance while judging several years ago. There is a spillway, where the aroma of a beer is intense, but not overwhelming, about one inch above the rim of a drinking vessel.. I call the area a sweetspot. Sniffing from that point will not overload the nose's scent receptors, and you can merrily sniff away to your heart's content. The scent can actually be felt inside the nose, much like a soft breeze on the skin.

Most beer should have a clean or nearly clean aroma/odor, without any traces of infection or other problems. Murphy's has a clean aroma/odor.

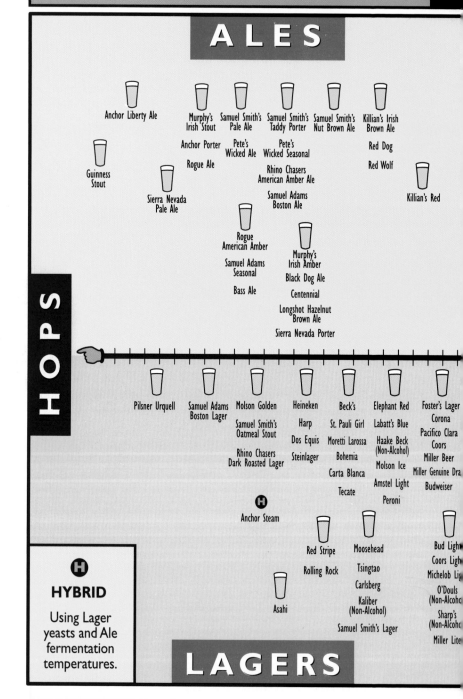

Some of the beers Bennigan's features in the Copper Clover International Beer Quest are charted below to help you see at a glance the variety of beer tastes and styles offered.

ALES

Anchor Liberty Ale

Murphy's Irish Stout
Samuel Smith's Pale Ale
Samuel Smith's Taddy Porter
Samuel Smith's Nut Brown Ale
Killian's Irish Brown Ale

Anchor Porter
Pete's Wicked Ale
Pete's Wicked Seasonal
Red Dog

Guinness Stout
Rogue Ale
Rhino Chasers American Amber Ale
Red Wolf

Sierra Nevada Pale Ale
Samuel Adams Boston Ale
Killian's Red

Rogue American Amber

Murphy's Irish Amber

Samuel Adams Seasonal
Black Dog Ale

Bass Ale
Centennial

Longshot Hazelnut Brown Ale

Sierra Nevada Porter

HOPS

Pilsner Urquell

Samuel Adams Boston Lager

Molson Golden
Heineken
Beck's
Elephant Red
Foster's Lager

Samuel Smith's Oatmeal Stout
Harp
St. Pauli Girl
Labatt's Blue
Corona

Dos Equis
Moretti Larossa
Haake Beck (Non-Alcohol)
Pacifico Clara

Rhino Chasers Dark Roasted Lager
Steinlager
Bohemia
Molson Ice
Coors

Carta Blanca
Amstel Light
Miller Beer

Tecate
Peroni
Miller Genuine Dra

Budweiser

Ⓗ Anchor Steam

Red Stripe
Moosehead
Bud Light

Rolling Rock
Tsingtao
Coors Ligh

Carlsberg
Michelob Li

Asahi
Kaliber (Non-Alcohol)
O'Douls (Non-Alcoho

Samuel Smith's Lager
Sharp's (Non-Alcoho

Miller Lite

Ⓗ HYBRID
Using Lager yeasts and Ale fermentation temperatures.

LAGERS

REMEMBER: Ales are fermented at a higher temperature and at the top of the brewing tank. Lagers ferment at a lower temperature at the bottom of the brewing tank.

ALES

Hoegarden White

Lindemans Framboise

Black Dog
Honey Rasberry Ale

Killian's
Wilde Honey

Pete's Wicked
Honey Wheat

Rhino Chasers
Honey Wheat

Samuel Adams
Scotch Ale

Samuel Adams
Honey Porter

M A L T

Beck's Dark

Hacker-Pschorr
Munich Edelhell

Negra Modelo

Michelob Amber Bock

Hacker-Pschorr
Weisse

Longshot
Black Lager

Paulaner Salvator
Dopplebock

LAGERS

I awarded the full five points.

Note: from experience, I have noticed that almost every commercial beer will score either a four or a five in the first three judging categories.

First taste for body (5pt)

Now it's time to take that first sip of beer. Keep your mouth closed, at first, and swirl the beer all round inside your mouth so all surfaces are coated. This step is positioned in the sequence so that the taster can not only check the body of the beer, but also line the mouth with beer, which will aid in the following step. What we want to determine in this step is the consistency of the beer. Yes, beer is liquid, but not all liquids have the same denseness, viscosity, or body. Water is considered thin. Maple syrup is considered fairly thick, but not as thick as molasses, which isn't as thick as tooth-paste. Beer doesn't have that broad a spectrum, but it serves to illustrate the point about body. The presence of higher alcohol levels will also appear at this step. You should be able to feel its warming effects at levels above 5.5–6% ABV. At levels greater than 8.5–9.0% ABV, alcoholic warming is very evident at the back of the mouth and into the upper throat.

Stouts should be relatively full-bodied. I find Murphy's just a little less than optimum.

I awarded four points.

First aroma/bouquet perception (5pt)

Now we take another sniff of the beer just above the rim, as I previously explained. This time we are not trying to determine if the beer has a clean nose, or not, but what specific elements or notes are in the nose. Hops and malt are the obvious first things to sniff out. You will usually find one or the other is dominant, sometimes to the total exclusion of the other. For example, in the case of Murphy's Stout, the beautiful malt, roast barley, and biscuit notes completely overwhelms any hop aromas, though certainly a lot of hops were used in the copper to counterbalance the malts, especially the chocolate, black patent, and roast barley. This beer's nose is lovely.

I awarded the full five points.

Carbonation-character (after the first taste) (5pt)

Take a second sip now. Continue to mull over the aromas you've just discovered, but now concentrate on the amount of fizziness the beer lays on your tongue. Keep your mouth closed at first, and swirl the beer all round, as before. Then swallow, and draw air into your mouth. You should feel the carbon dioxide in the beer fizzing all over your tongue (and the insides of your cheeks). The intensity of the feeling is what we seek to assess. A highly carbonated wheat beer, or a Pilsner will be really fizzy. A Barleywine will seem almost flat. Note that most ales, especially those from the British Isles, have low to only moderate carbonation. I found Murphy's Stout to be fizzy, and somewhat lively, without being overwhelming, but not as much as I expect in a Stout.

I gave it four points.

Hop/malt balance (5pt)

Take a third sip (or fourth, if you double-sipped at any of the previous tasting stages). The balance between hops and malt in every beer is important, especially when held against style parameters. Some beers initially start out malt, then quickly lose the malt, as hop bitterness asserts itself. Other's react in an opposite manner. Sometimes the hops and malt quickly reach equilibrium. Each beer will have a different balance, and take a different route to reach it. Recall that there are three stages at which one assesses the notes a beer leaves on the palate. The initial stage occurs almost immediately after one takes a sip. The second stage kicks in after one has swallowed, and then drawn air into the mouth. This typically lasts a few minutes. The second stage is very interesting because so much can happen during it. One could think of the third stage as a battlefield upon which malt and hops slug it out. The third stage is called the finish. Malt is dominant, and maintains this position, until the finish turns slightly dry, in Murphy's Stout.

I awarded the full five points.

Finish (quality) (5pt)

Time for another sip. The quality of the finish is how well all the different tastes in a beer get along on the palate. Harmony is a word that could be used in describing what we are looking for in this stage. Any taste notes that disturb the harmony of tastes detracts from the quality of the finish. For instance, too much hop bitterness, astringency, residual sweetness, alcohol levels, or any other taste, degrades the quality of the finish.

I found Murphy's Stout to have a fine finish, just off the mark, but it is so good it is easy to drink more than one of them.

I awarded four points.

Overall impression (10pt)

At this stage you are on your own to award points based on how much you liked the beer. However, bear in mind that you should still consider the style parameters of the beer when making this final assessment. What happens on occasion is that you will find the beer truly delicious, yet the brewer missed the style mark at one or more stages. You could make a note, as I do, that the beer was great-tasting, but was too hoppy and dry for the style. I will mark the beer down here, and not give it as many points as the overall taste might warrant.

Though I gave Murphy's Stout four points in three steps, I felt the beer so close to the optimum that I gave it nine points.

My scores, I gave an overall mark of 46 points, an Excellent grade.

Sampling sequences to discern tastes, styles

To provide a quick and easy way to learn about beer styles and distinguish tastes, I've selected three suggested sampling sequences – different assortments of four beers each and group in various ways. I chose one beer from a group that I used as an example to previously illustrate the process (see page 41). You, of course, should choose whichever group strikes your fancy.

For taste sequencing such as this, consider using 3 to 4 ounce samples of each. Bennigan's offers such samples of their draft beer. For the bottled beer groups, share a single bottle among three or four friends.

Wide selection sampling sequence

Beer styles are spread across a broad spectrum of colors, tastes and ingredients. Therefore, I have selected beers from Bennigan's long beer list to illustrate the variety of styles. Four styles, Lager, Weisse, Vienna, and Stout, and four countries, Denmark, Germany, Ireland and the Mexico are represented here. The drinking order is from light to dark, the Stout coming last so it doesn't overwhelm the others.

Carlsberg Lager typical northern European lager, is often referred to as Continental Light. The Carlsberg concern is one of the largest in the world. Its brands are produced under licence or directly in over a dozen countries besides its Copenhagen home. Its brands come under a wide variety of names, and in differing alcohol strengths. Carlsberg Lager throws a nice thick head. Initially, it is malt-dominant that gives ground to the hop. There are smooth, soft, malty notes on the palate, with some hop dryness in the finish.

Hacker-Pschorr Weisse is from one of Munich's leading breweries. Originally it was independent, but merged, and then were taken over by Paulaner, another Munich brewery. Hacker-Pschorr Weisse is a fine example of southern German wheat beer. Pale in color, it throws a huge head, and is very lively in the glass and on the tongue. The nose if full of clove notes, and there are tart apple, grainy, biscuit notes on the palate that blend nicely with an underlying sweetness. The finish is fruity.

Dos Equis, from the Moctezuma brewery in Mexico, is a widely available and well known example of the Vienna style. Its color is amber-red, and its body lies between that of a Continental Light and a Märzen. The taste is mild in the nose and palate, making it an easy-drinking beer.

Murphy's Stout, brewed in an 1850s brewery, is from Cork, Ireland. The firm is now owned by Heineken, the second largest brewer in the world. Murphy's Stout throws a large, tan, thick head that laces the glass. This is a soft, malty rendition of classic Irish Stout, which tend to be much hoppier. It has distinctive roasty and chocolate notes on the palate, and a long mellow finish.

Pale Ale sampling sequence

The beers for the Pale Ale group were chosen to show the way different brewers interpret a style. In this case, the style is split between an English Pale Ale, and three North American interpretations.

Pale Ale is a group for those who love the hop. There is hop in the nose, hop in the palate, and drinking these will put hop in your dreams. I chose it because this style has its emphasis on hops, which will allow you to easily identify it in the nose and palate.

Anchor Liberty Ale, from the brewery of the same name in San Francisco, is a hop-lovers delight. The nose is intensely aromatic from the use of Cascade hops, which often also gives a grapefruit note on the palate. The finish is dry. At 6.0% ABV, you should also sense some alcohol warming at the back of the throat. This beer is oft imitated by others.

Samuel Smith's Pale Ale is a Yorkshire, England, classic. The basis for this beer is a cask-conditioned Museum Ale brand sold in Britain. Of the four in this group, this is the least hoppy, but is an excellent example of how some English brewers think of Pale Ale.

Sierra Nevada Pale Ale is the bottled version of Sierra Nevada Draught Ale, and even more highly regarded. The Pale Ale is a North American classic. As with many West Coast brewers, Cascade hops feature prominently. Their floral notes combine nicely with fruity notes from the yeast. Some malt notes in the nose are perceptible. The finish is moderately dry, but not by too much.

Rogue Ale is from a brewery in Newport, Oregon. This smooth-drinking example takes an opposite tack than other West Coast breweries in that the hopping is more Kent Goldings than Cascade or other Pacific Northwest-grown hops – in other words, is more moderate. Its English nature is most evident in the finish, where it is noteworthy. There is a nice balance between hops and malt on the palate, again, more in the English custom than the North American. Body is medium.

Draft beer sampling sequence

To many, nothing beats a draft beer. I have assembled four from Bennigan's draft offerings, which number 15–20 at most locations.

Bass Ale, the classic from Burton-upon-Trent, England, is considered the epitomy of all Pales Ales. Challenger, Goldings, and Northdown hops are used. They give this beer its complex nose. There is pronounced malt in the body, which stiffens it, and in the palate, where it gives way to a long delicate finish, with light apple notes. Though the brewing process has undergone some changes, this high-quality beer is still complex and well-rounded. Alcohol content is about 5.0% ABV.

Pete's Wicked Seasonal is one of a steadily increasing number of beers grouped together under this heading. Because, as with Grand Crus, there are no parameters, these beers are not of a particular style. Pete's winter seasonal brew has lovely spicy notes in both the nose and palate with nutmeg being the most prominent. It's color is a fairly deep brown. For a spiced beer, which can be somewhat cloying on the palate, this one is fresh-tasting, mellow, and smooth.

Samuel Adams Seasonal is one of a long line of beers from the number one contract brewery in North America. Sam Adams beers are all known for their distinctive noses and appropriately-full bodies. The label bland has never been hung on a beer from this growing concern, and rightly so. Their deep red-amber colored Winter Lager is a big beer in every sense. The nose is full of spicy, malty, and caramel notes. The body is big. Some malted wheat is used, which gives this beer a crisp, clean finish. Five different hops varieties are used. They help give the beer a delightful nose. Alcohol content varies from year to year, as does its recipe. It was introduced in 1989.

Guinness Stout is considered the classic of the style, and the one everybody knows. It certainly is the driest and most complex of Stouts. Too, its color is opaque black due to the high levels of roasted barley used. It's one of the darkest beers available. There are actually several different versions, all with different alcohol content and character. The draft version has about 4.25 ABV, and the head is aided by nitrogen in the dispense line.

Sampling wrap-up

Well, there they are. Twelve beers in three groups, selected to give you a well-balanced introduction into some of the many beer styles, and their interesting and delicious tastes. Now you can experiment putting together your own group tastings. Take advantage of the great opportunity presented to you by Bennigan's through their long and varied Copper Clover International Beer Quest list. I believe you will find the Quest well worth taking. As you journey further along it, you will learn more and more about the beverage we all love best–beer!

Chapter 3

Beer tasters' toasts

THE CUSTOM OF drinking healths and pledging has been called toasting in the English-speaking world since the 1700s. The word is well-connected to the British custom of putting toast, often spiced, in their ale mugs and wine glasses. The two quotes immediately below are citations of the earliest English-language references to toasts, in the usage here.

In Shakespeare's *Merry Wives of Windsor,* we have the line: *"Go fetch me a quart of sack! Put toast in't."* (*Sack* being wine.)

During the reign of Charles II, the Earl of Rochester wrote:
Make it so large that, filled with Sack
Up to the swelling brim,
Vast toasts on the delicious lake,
Like ships at sea, may swim.

Toasts should be either amusing or touching, never embarrassing, and be no longer than a minute.

Finally, non-drinkers should not turn their glasses upside down but, rather, raise empty ones. Etiquette dictates you stand for a toast when everyone else does.

National toasts

England: *Good health, Cheers, Bottoms up*
Finland: *Maljanne* (Here's to you!), *kippis* (Cheers)
France: *A votre sante!* (To your health!), *Bon Sante!* (Good health!)
Germany: *Prosit* (Your Health), *Prost* (Bavarian variation of *prosit*), *Trink zu!* (Bottoms up).
Ireland: *Air do Slainte* (To your good health). It is some times shortened to *Slainte.*
Italy: *Alla salute viva moi!* (Good health–viva ourselves)
Netherlands: *Gezondheid!* (Good health)
Russia: *Nastrovia* (To your health)
Scotland: *Slainthe eh–uit doch slainthe eh laut!* (Hail to you. A toast to your good health.)
Sweden: *Skaal!* (Your health)
Switzerland: *Gsundtheit!* (Good health!)
United States: Here's to you, Cheers, Prosit, Prost; Bottoms up. Toasts in the States are given in many different tongues.
Wales: *Iechyd d I chwi!* (Your health in drinking)

Birthdays

**May the friendship and happiness,
We celebrate today, on your birthday,
Be with you every day this year**

Here's to true friends, who join me again this year,
To celebrate my 39th one more time,
Without calling attention,
To my inability to count.

May your birthday mark the birth
Of another great adventure in your life

To my good friend who learned years ago
That birthdays are celebrations, not of years of age,
But of youthful spirit.
May you continue to be young at heart.

Sporting events

Let's salute our team's winning spirit,
And declare the game's score irrelevant

May we all remember that winning is giving 100%,
Which is not always reflected in the scoreboard

We came. We played. We gave it our best.
Now that's worthy of a toast.

 **You win some. You lose some.**
And there's always next season.
Let's drink to that.

May we remember the sweetness of this victory,
Should we someday be stung by the bitterness of defeat.

Friendship

Here's to eternity.
May we spend it in as good company as this night finds us.

Here's to our best friends, who know the worst about us,
But refuse to believe it.

May you live to be a hundred years,
with one extra year to repent.

May the roof above us never fall in,
And may we friends gathered below never fall out.

May I live one hundred years,
And you a hundred and a day,
That I should never hear the news,
That sadly you had passed away.

May we have a few real friends,
Rather than a thousand acquaintances.

Weddings & marriage

May the joy you feel today be but a pale shadow,
Of that which is to come.

"Nothing is nobler, nor more admirable,
Than when two people who see eye-to-eye,
Live together as husband and wife;
Thereby confounding their enemies,
And delighting their friends."
–Homer, from The Odyessy

**As you set out to write a new chapter in your life,
As husband and wife,
May your union be like a game of poker:
Start as a pair, and end with a full house!**

To the Bride and Groom,
Three things to remember.
Things are more like they are today,
Than they ever have been before.
The facts, although interesting are irrelevant.
And finally, by the time you can make ends meet,
They move the ends.

Health and long life to you,
The woman of your choice to you,
A child every year to you,
Land without rent to you,
And may you die in Ireland.

**May the rest of your lives be like a bed of red roses...
without the thorns.**

**May your love be as deep as the ocean,
And your troubles as light as the foam.**

May you be poor in misfortune,
Rich in blessings,
Slow to make enemies,
Quick to make friends;
But rich or poor, quick or slow;
May you know nothing but happiness,
From this day forward.

Here's to the husband.
Here's to the wife.
May they remain lovers for life.

May your life together be as happy and free
As the rolling waves on the deep blue sea.

May you share a joy that grows deeper,
A friendship that grows closer,
And a marriage that grows richer through the years.
Cheers!

To love and laughter and happily ever after.

Here's to a long life,
And a happy one.
Here's to a good wife,
And a faithful one.
Here's to a swift death,
And a painless one.

**Here's to a good beer,
And another one!**

May your good times be plenty,
And your sad times be few;
May your love grow brighter with each day,
And with each day begin anew;
~~Let us~~ live for the future,
~~And~~ learn from the past;
~~Because the knowledge you~~ gain,
Will ~~make your marriage~~ last.

next pas.

**To Fate, that brought you together,
And to Love, that will keep you happy forever.**

**To a couple destined for a world of success;
Not only in life, but in love.
Congratulations, and good luck, my friends.**

May your love be modern enough to survive the Times,
And old fashioned enough to last Forever.

May you never lie, cheat or drink,
But if you must lie, lie in each others arms,
And if you must cheat, cheat death,
But if you must drink, drink with all of us,
Because we love you.

Anniversaries

May the joy of your wedding day,
Be multiplied for each anniversary accordingly.

Here's to you both,
A beautiful pair;
On this, the birthday,
Of your love affair!

May each year be the best year of your marriage.

Families

To our family...
We don't have the opportunity,
To pick the family we're born into.
But if I had the opportunity, you can be sure,
You're the family I'd choose.

To brothers and sisters...
Whose hours of childhood pranks,
Now provide hours of comic relief,
At family reunions.

To my parents...
Who usually had all the answers,
When I was growing up;
And who also had the patience and wisdom,
Not to act like it.

To my brother (sister)
May your children be as quick to forget the quarrels,
And as slow to forget the happy memories,
As we have all these years.

Here's to you and yours and to mine and ours;
And if mine and ours ever come across you and yours;
I hope you and yours will do as much for mine and ours;
As mine and ours have done for you and yours.

Seasonal and holidays

New Year's Day

Here's to the new year,
And setting a new record for keeping resolutions

May your problems be as long-lived,
As my new year's Resolutions.

May this new year bring you more happiness,
Than all your others combined.

I wish you a Merry Christmas,
And a Happy New Year!
A pocket full of money,
And a cellar full of beer!

Be at war with your voices,
At peace with your neighbors,
And let every new year find you a better man.
(Benjamin Franklin)

In the new year, may your right hand always be stretched
out in friendship, but never in want.

Valentine's Day

Here's to the best Valentine gift–your company

May every day be Valentine's Day for us.

St Patrick's Day

**May the luck of the Irish be with you,
Today and every day.**

May this day of celebration,
Chase away your worries,
Just as St Patrick chased the snakes out of Ireland.

**St. Patrick was a gentleman,
Who through strategy and stealth
Drove all the snakes from Ireland;
Heres a toasting to his health;
But not too many toastings,
Lest you lose yourself,
And then forget the good St Patrick,
And see all those snakes again.**

Halloween

On this night of Trick and Treat,
May your treats be many,
And your tricks few.

**Here's to your costume on Halloween,
May it be the best contest judges have seen.**

Thanksgiving

May we always take time to be thankful,
And help those with needs more bountiful.

Here's to the early pilgrims on U.S. banks,
For establishing a tradition of giving thanks.

Career events

Here's to your promotion...
May we celebrate your rise,
To new heights of achievement.

May your service to the company over the past ten years,
Be returned to you in kind.

May you navigate your new career choice,
As adeptly as you sailed through this one.

Here's to the adventures of your new job.
May your pathway be a rewarding one,
And may you return from time to time,
To celebrate with colleagues,
You met along the way.

Here's to record achievements (sales, production, etc)
May these form the baseline on our growth charts,
For years to follow.

Let us welcome the newest member of our team.
May he (she) soon feel at home among friends and family.

Assorted toasts

May those that love us, Love us.
And those that don't love us,
May God turn their heart;
And if He doesn't turn their hearts,
May he turn their ankles
So we'll know them by their limping.

Here's a health to your enemy's enemies.

May the road rise to meet you;
May the wind be always at your back;
The sun shine warm upon your face;
The rain fall soft upon your fields;
And until we meet again,
May God hold you in the hollow of his hand.

May our feast days be many and our fast days be few.

May you have the strength to change,
Those things that can be changed;
May you have the patience to live,
With those things that cannot be changed;
May you have the wisdom,
To know one from the other!

May the face of every good news,
And the back of every bad news,
Be toward us.

May all your troubles be little ones.

Here's to life. It's something to do.

**May your hands be forever clasped in friendship,
And your hearts forever joined in love**

Here's that we may always have a clean shirt,
A clean conscience,
And a guinea in our pocket.

May you have warm words on a cold evening,
A full moon on a dark night,
And the road downhill all the way to your door.

May there be a generation of children,
On the children of your children.

**May the most you ever wish for,
Be the least you ever receive.**

May you live as long as you want to,
And want to as long as you live.

**All that we have drank, sang, and danced,
No one can ever take away from us.**

May all of your days be as happy as the ones before.

A little health, a little wealth,

May your coffins be made of 100 year-old oak,
That was planted today.

May you live a long, happy life,
And may my voice be the last one you hear.

Chapter 4

Food & beer matches
Great food & beer tips

BEER HAS HELD a place of honor at mankind's table for thousands of years. Many have tried to displace it in favor of wine, but they not succeeded. Wine, long the center stage attraction in culinary circles throughout the world, is now sharing the spotlight with beer if not stepping aside for star performing brews. For example, the Culinary Institute of America, Hyde Park, NY, has held sold-out beer dinners over the past several years, without as much as a drop of wine in the dining room.

Beer has had more attention paid to it in the last six years than in the preceding 90. Look at the proliferation of brew publications, space devoted to beer in mainstream magazines and newspapers, and broadcast time covering beer on television and radio. And today, beer books have their own ever-growing section in book stores.

Although much has been written in the last few years about beer and food, beer connoissuers haven't developed hard and fast rules about matching beer to foods. Unlike wine with its once-strict etiquette for red with beef and white with poultry and fish, beer enthusiasts are more relaxed about combining beer and food. The most important rule of etiquette, if you want to call it that: **Experiment to find the taste combinations you like.** After all, that's the fun of exploring the new world of beers.

To help you discover your favorite taste combinations, here are some general suggestions to start with:

Complement tastes:

Match the intensity and character of flavor profiles for both beer and foods. The key here is balance, just like the hops and malt balance in beers to give it pleasing taste. The beer shouldn't overwhelm the food, and the food shouldn't overshadow the beer. Lighter foods such as grilled shrimp and vegetables are framed nicely with the light, crisp flavors of Rolling Rock lager. Hearty foods such as steak or chops pair nicely with a dark ale such as Samuel Smith's Nut Brown Ale. Character flavors of pasta marinara dishes invite the flavorful Italian influences Peroni or Moretti Larossa beers. Robust food profiles including smoked meats and spicy Cajun, Oriental or Indian entrees are complemented with robust flavored beers such as Rhino Chasers Dark Roasted Lager, Samuel Adams Boston Lager or Anchor Steam.

Contrast tastes:

At the same time, consider opposite flavor profile pairings such as the dry hoppy taste of a Sierra Nevada Pale Ale or Pilsner Urquell with the sweet flavor of an Oriental chicken salad. Reversing the flavor profiles, try a flavored beer such as a Killians Wilde Honey with a club salad.

Quenching factors:

When enjoying extremely hot and spicy foods, beer comes to the rescue of your taste buds by providing a quenching, cooling flavor experience. Next time you choose a fiery hot platter of Buffalo Wings, enjoy a Paulaner Hefe Weizen, Red Stripe, Molson Ice or Ice House.

Palate Cleansing:

Beer can enhance your dining experience by serving as a refreshing way to cleanse your palate after enjoying fried appetizers, such as Bennigan's Broccoli Bites or Fried Mushrooms, and before moving on to your salad or entree. Several nice brews to accompany fried foods are Rolling Rock Lager and Asahi Pilsner.

Even with these guidelines, your best bet is to experiment. Share different types of beer with friends to expand your taste experiences, and to allow you to taste different beers with different foods.

Obviously, an establishment with a long beer list presents many combinations and choices. A place with a list that is wholly comprised of Standard Lager really offers one no choice at all.

Bennigan's offers a wonderful opportunity for guests to explore a multitude of beer and food tastes. One of the things that made Bennigan's so popular over the years was that it offered a truly huge selection of food – from appetizers to entrees. Today that is still the case. Responding again to consumer taste preferences, Bennigan's has expanded its beer offerings. In doing so, Bennigan's has given guests what they wanted: a place where they could combine specialty beer tastes with great food tastes.

To illustrate, three menu items are especially interesting and delicious, both alone and when combined with a matching beer. From the appetizer list, Chicken Quesadillas are a stand-out. Spicy fajita chicken, onions, melted colby and jack cheeses are folded between flour tortillas, then grilled and served with guacamole, sour cream and salsa. Combine this taste combination with hop-dominant beer styles such as India Pale Ale, Pilsner, Vienna or Wheat Beer, to cut through the zesty flavors, and you've got a mouthful of stimulating tastes. From the sandwich list, try the Pretzel Roll Reuben™. The pretzel rolls are really rich in texture and taste. Combine it with malt-dominant styles such as Bock, Märzen, Doppelbock or Scotch ale. The malt sweetness, heavier bodies and increased alcohol content of these styles can easily handle the corned beef, Swiss cheese and sauerkraut of this sandwich. For dessert, one of my favorites is the Brownie Bottom Pie. I have a sweet-tooth longer than a sabre-tooth tiger fang. Try this with a Belgian Frambozenbier. The rasberry fruit in this beer is the perfect complement to all the rich chocolate in the pie.

The following list is but one of suggestions. I've selected some of the some of the most popular Bennigan's menu items, to match with some interesting beers. I've indicated beer styles as well as an example brand representative of that style. Use them as a starting point, then experiment on your own. *Bon appetit!*

Appetizers

Bennigan's Best Sampler: *a tempting combination of Bennigan's famous Buffalo Wings, Potato Skins and Fried Cheese. Served with marina sauce, blue cheese dressing and sour cream.* Lagers: Harp or Heineken

Spectacular Spinach Artichoke Dip: *a cream spinich dip garnished with sour cream and salsa. Served with tortilla chips.* Pale Ale (Sierra Nevada); Vienna (Dos Equis)

Burgers

Big flavors of burgers are perfect companions for the malty richness of dark ales and lagers. Choices of toppings may vary your selection of brews for pairing.

Bacon and Swiss: *melted Swiss cheese and crisp bacon slices, mayonnaise and all the trimmings are piled on this burger.* Steam (Anchor Old Foghorn); Doppelbock (Paulaner Salvator)

Southwest Burger: *a combination of peppers and onions, topped with melted cheddar cheese, Ranch dressing, Cholula hot sauce, lettuce and tomato.* Brown Ale (Pete's Wicked Ale); Pilsner (Tecate)

Salads

Monte Cristo: *ham and turkey with Swiss and American cheeses on wheat bread, battered and fried 'til golden, then sprinkled with powdered sugar. Served with red raspberry preserves.* Fruited beer (Lindemans Framboise); Brown Ale (Samuel Smith Nut Brown Ale)

Swiss Chicken Sandwich: *a grilled breast topped with sauteed*

mushrooms, melted Swiss cheese, mayonnaise and all the trimmings
Light Lager (Amstel Light); Pale Ale (Sierra Nevada)

Bennigan's Health Club™

Non-alcohol or low alcohol beers are a good match for food items in this section. Alcohol is the main contributor of calories in beer. But just in case you plan to splurge a few calories on brews, we've included additional suggestions.

Health Club Chicken Platter: *two fajita-marinated chicken breasts, charbroiled and served with our spicy confetti rice and fresh steam broccoli.*
Non-Alcohol (O'Douls or Sharp's); Light (Amstel Light)

Health Club Club Sandwich: *a combination of turkey, ham and low-fat jalapeno jack cheese with lettuce, tomato and no-fat mustardaise on whole wheat bread. Served with carrot and celery sticks and no-fat Ranch dressing.*
Non-Alcohol (Kaliber); Pilsner (Beck's); Lager (Heineken)

Health Club Vegetable Lasagna: *deep-dish vegetable lasagna, topped with marinara sauce and served with steamed broccoli.*
Non-Alcohol (Haake Beck); Continental Lager (Moretti Larossa)

Entrees

Cyprus Chicken Pasta: *Mediterranean-style chicken breast atop fettuccine with pine nuts, calamata olives and tomatoes, sautéed in olive oil and topped with parmesan cheese.*
Lager (Carlsberg); Wheat Beer (Pete's Wicked Honey)

Fajitas: *authentic Santa Fe style with strips of grilled chicken and tender beef sizzling among onions and red and green peppers. Served with a side dish of guacamole, sour cream, colby cheese, lettuce and tomatoes.*
Pilsner (Bohemia or Tecate); Dark Lager (Rhino Chasers Dark Roasted)

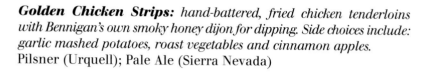

Golden Chicken Strips: *hand-battered, fried chicken tenderloins with Bennigan's own smoky honey dijon for dipping. Side choices include: garlic mashed potatoes, roast vegetables and cinnamon apples.*
Pilsner (Urquell); Pale Ale (Sierra Nevada)

Pot of Gold Pot Roast: *tender chuck roast with seasoned red potatoes, carrots, celery and onions in gravy. Served with fresh-baked roll.*
Brown Ale (Samuel Smith's Nut Brown); Scotch Ale (McEwan's)

Bennigan's BBQ Platter: *Baby Back Ribs and a charbroiled BBQ chicken breast. Served with cole slaw and crispy French fries.*
Stout: (Guinness); Porter (Murphy's Irish)

Desserts

Death By Chocolate®: *Bennigan's original recipe of chocolate-covered Rocky Road and Dutch Chocolate ice cream, mixed with Twix® Cookie Bars on a cookie crust. Pour on a side of hot chocolate topping.*
Doppelbock (Paulaner Salvator); Strong dark lager: (Rhino Chasers); Fruit (Lindemans Framboise); Stout (Guinness); Brown Ale (Long Shot Hazelnut Brown)

Abbey's Apple Sizzler: *a generous skillet, lined with an oatmeal cookie crust, then piled high with hot cinnamon apples mixed with raisins.*
Wheat (Samuel Adams Cherry Wheat or Pete's Honey Wheat)

Bennigan's Beer Menu

Australia
61 Foster's Special Bitter
Continental Light Lager

Belgum
46 Lindemans Framboise
Fruited Lambic

Canada
160 Elephant Red
Continental Light Lager

26 Labatt's Blue
North American Standard

27 Molson Golden
North American Standard

28 Molson Ice
North American Ice

29 Moosehead
North American Standard

China
85 Tsingtao
Continental Lager

Czech Republic
80 Pilsner Urquell
Czech Pilsner

Denmark
25 Carlsberg
Continental/European Lager

England
301 Kaliber (Non-Alcohol)
NABLAB

54 Samuel Smith's Nut
Brown Ale
Brown Ale

55 Samuel Smith's Oatmeal
Stout *Oatmeal Stout*

56 Samuel Smith's Pale Ale
Pale Ale

Germany
18 Beck's Dark
Continental Dark Lager

393 Haake Beck (Non-Alcohol)
NABLAB

103 Hacker-Pschorr Munich
Edelhell
Bavarian Helles

104 Hacker-Pschorr Weisse
Weisse

59 Paulaner Hefe-Weizen
Weisse

52 Paulaner Salvator
Dopplebock
Dopplebock

16 St. Pauli Girl
Continental Lager

Holland
13 Heineken
Continental Lager

Ireland
2 Harp
Continental Lager

258 Murphy's Irish Stout
Stout

Italy
78 Moretti Larossa
Continental Lager - Light

84 Peroni
Continental Lager - Light

Jamaica
1 Red Stripe
Continental Lager - Light

Japan
24 Asahi
Continental Lager - Light

Mexico
89 Bohemia
North American Pils

8 Carta Blanca
North American Standard

19 Corona
North American Standard

23 Dos Equis
Vienna

20 Negra Modelo
Continental Dark Lager

21 Pacifico Clara
North American Standard

9 Tecate
Vienna

New Zealand
3 Steinlager
Continental Lager

USA
146 Anchor Liberty Ale
Pale Ale - North American

86 Anchor Steam
*Hybrid -
California Common*

102 Black Dog Ale
Pale Ale - North American

197 Black Dog Honey
Raspberry Ale
*Specialty Beer -
North American*

NOTE: Core beer menu; additional beers will vary region to region

USA

40 Coors
American Standard

41 Coors Light *Low Cal -*
North American Standard

42 Icehouse
Ice - North American

162 Killian's Irish Brown Ale
Brown Ale -
North American

32 Killian's Red
Pale Ale - North American

334 Killian's Wilde Honey
Specialty - North American

386 Longshot Hazelnut
Brown Ale
Specialty - North American

220 Michelob Amber Bock
Bock - North American

742 Michelob Golden Pilsner
Pilsner - North American

225 Michelob Light
Light Lager -
North American

316 Miller Beer
Premium - North American

43 Miller Genuine Draft
Premium Lager -
N. American

304 O'Douls (Non-Alcohol)
NABLAB

236 Pete's Wicked Honey
Wheat *Specialty -*
North American

DRAFT BEERS

England
95 Bass Ale *Pale Ale*

Germany
17 Beck's
Continental Lager

Holland
12 Amstel Light
Continental Lager

Ireland
98 Guinness Stout *Stout*

306 Murphy's Irish Amber
Irish Amber

USA
39 Bud Light
Low Calorie North American

96 Budweiser
Standard Lager

99 Miller Lite
Low Calorie North American

7 Pete's Wicked Ale
Brown Ale North
American Craft

208 Pete's Wicked Seasonal
Seasonal Specialty

14 Samuel Adams Boston
Lager
Dortmunder Export

94 Samuel Adams Seasonal
Seasonal Specialty

38 Red Dog
Premium Lager

100 Red Wolf
Premium Lager

49 Rhino Chasers American
Amber Ale *Pale Ale -*
North American Craft

423 Rhino Chasers Dark
Roasted Lager
Dark Lager -
North American Craft

409 Rhino Chasers Peach
Honey Wheat
Specialty - North American

72 Rogue Ale
Pale Ale - English

237 Rogue American Amber
Pale Ale -
North American Craft

37 Rolling Rock
Premium Lager -
North American

157 Samuel Adams Cherry
Wheat *Specialty*

314 Samuel Adams Golden
Pilsner *Pils - Germany*

108 Samuel Adams Honey
Porter *Specialty*

584 Sharp's (Non-Alcoholic)
NABLAB

87 Sierra Nevada Pale Ale
North American Craft

88 Sierra Nevada Porter
Porter -
North American Craft

NOTE: Core beer menu; additional beers will vary region to region

Chapter 5

Information
Restaurant locations
Tap Time™

Copper Clover International Beer Quest®

Bennigan's, the leading restaurant company which helped establish casual dining in America, now offers an international beer experience unlike any other. With more than 100 beers, Bennigan's invites you to celebrate their tastes, and satisfy your curiosity about brews from around the world.

Enjoy the renaissance of specialty beers. Track your taste experiences electronically, and learn about the diverse world of beer styles. Experiment with different food and brew combinations. Pick up some beer trivia to entertain and challenge your friends. Celebrate your taste quest milestones. And join an exclusive group of Copper Clover International Beer Quest members who appreciate the adventure of exploring a beverage that's been a part of our culture for more than 8,ooo years.

Here's how the Copper Clover works.

Membership is free. Upon joining the Copper Clover International Beer Quest, you will receive a special membership card, much like a debit or credit card, which allows automated tracking of your progress at any Bennigan's location. Bennigan's is the first to offer automated tracking at multiple locations throughout the country, making your Quest more convenient and accessible, even when you are out of town.

As a Copper Clover International Beer Quest member, you will enjoy many exclusive membership benefits, including a newsletter, and beer style educational opportunities.

In states where prizes are permitted, milestones you achieve during your Quest will be recognized with prizes such as T-shirts, hats, gift certificates, and a Bennigan's True Pint™ glass.

Completing the Copper Quest

At the completion of your Quest to taste 100 different beers, your name will be engraved on a copper plate and attached to a plaque at the bar. You will also receive a copper membership card, entitling you to be served draft beer in a Copper True Pint™ glass in our restaurant.

Gold and Platinum Quests

For those who venture to explore and complete a second tier of 100 beers, you will receive a gold membership card, have your name engraved on a plate attached to the bar, and will be served draft beer in a gold True Pint™ glass.

After completing Quest number three, tasting 300 different varieties of beer, members will receive a platinum membership card, and will be served draft beer in a platinum True Pint™ glass, in addition to being recognized with your name on a plate attached to the bar.

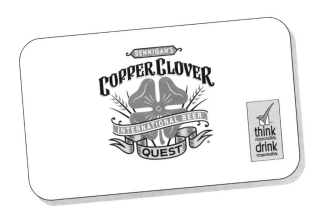

Tap Time™

REALIZING THAT A big part of the quest for higher knowledge about beer is sharing your newly acquired taste adventures with friends over some great-tasting foods, Bennigan's features Tap Time™ from 5–7 pm Monday through Friday. Bennigan's Tap Time provides an environment that fosters the socialization of beer and food adventures.

During Tap Time, a featured free appetizer bar offers the opportunity to explore the complementary and contrasting taste combinations of matching different beers with foods. Some of the delicious samplings on the free appetizer bar are featured on Bennigan's full menu, which focuses on unique tastes and fresh, home-made ingredients.

So, whether you're just learning to distinguish between lagers and ales, or you've recently discovered the difference between a witbier and a dunkel weizenbier, Bennigan's is designed for you. Bring your friends, or join the group at Bennigan's to share your newly-acquired beer knowledge, or debate the best brew for Buffalo Shrimp and Broccoli Bites.

True Pint™

IN TRUE IRISH pub fashion, all beer on tap is served in a True Pint™ glass–that's a full 16 ounces of refreshing brew.

In Britain, and elsewhere, by law, beer must be served in glasses with clearly indicated volume-marks, called 'lined glasses'. The liquid volume of beer must be at the line. Foam is discounted, and a drinker has the right to demand his pint (or litre) be topped up to the line. Government trading standards officers make frequent checks, and pubs found not complying with the law may be fined.

However, there is controversy around the entire issue, because the government reneged on a promise to implement the section of the weights and measures law that made selling short pints illegal.

The Brewer's Association guidelines say a pint has to be 95% liquid before the customer asks for a top-up. It is these guidelines that the inspectors are trying to enforce against governmental foot-dragging on the issue.

A recent check of pubs in Shropshire found only two pubs out of twenty five served a proper-measure pint. Over half served pints that were more than 5% short, and two pubs were serving pints that were 12.5% short. The latter shortchanged the drinker $0.30 per pint.

Part of the problem stemmed from the fact that the line was very near the rim of the glass, leaving little head. Compounding this publican's (tavernkeeper) nightmare was that many beer drinkers prefer a substantial head on their beer (this, a regional difference as much as an individual one). Should a publican serve a beer to a customer with a large head, as requested, he was breaking the law. If he obeyed the law, he had unhappy drinkers on his hands, or lost their custom. Oversized glasses, which allowed a full liquid measure plus a substantial head, were manufactured to solve the problem though they are not yet universally used in Britain.

One never hears of this in the States, where even the concept, of what a true pint serving actually is, is fuzzy. Bennigan's has taken the lead in the States, with the introduction of its True Pint™. Guests are assured a True Pint each and every time they order a draft beer–without the hassle of having to ask for a top-up.

Bennigan's restaurant directory

Please note that those restaurants printed with an (*) after the city name are not, at the time this book went to press, participating in the Copper Clover International Beer Quest program.

Alabama

Homewood	197 Vulcan Road 205.942.7410

Arizona

Mesa	1216 West Southern Avenue 602.898.3404
Phoenix	10051 East.Metro Parkway 602.943.7267

Arkansas

Little Rock	104 South University Avenue 501.664.8160

California

Arcadia*	400 East Huntington Avenue 818.445.1358
City of Industry*	1630 South Azusa Avenue 818.912.5780
Costa Mesa*	3333 Bristol Street 714.241.8938
Fullerton*	1401 South Harbor Boulevard 714.879.9324
Laguna Hills*	24231 Avenida de la Carlota 714.837.0340
Santa Clara	4150 Great America Parkway 408.748.0378
San Diego	1760 Camino Del Rio North 619.291.8853

Westminster*	545 Westminster Mall 714.891.4522

Colorado

Arvada	5390 Wadsworth Bypass 303.420.3965
Aurora	2710 South Havana Street 303.750.7822
Aurora	13950 East Mississippi 303.671.5040
Boulder	2550 Canyon Blvd 303.444.0147
Colorado Springs	3502 North Academy Boulevard 719.591.0303
Denver	1699 South Colorado Boulevard 303.753.0272
Englewood	9281 East Arapaho Road 303.792.0280
Fort Collins	2203 South College Avenue 303.484.7974
Lakewood	7425 West Alameda Avenue 303.233.5090
Lakewood	3601 South Wadsworth Boulevard 303.969.9955
Westminster	7605 West 88th Avenue 303.431.1696

Connecticut

Milford	290 Old Gate Lane 203.877.1903
Stamford	300 Atlantic Street 203.327.2801

Delaware

Newark	601 Ogletown Road 302.368.3333
Wilmington	2015 Concord Turnpike 302.652.8910

Florida

Altamonte Springs	244 West Highway 436
	407.862.7200
Boca Raton	2420 North Federal Highway
	407.391.1196
Bradenton	320 Cortez Road West
	941.753.6451
Brandon	2210 West Brandon Boulevard
	813.689.5226
Casselberry	1385 North Semoran Boulevard
	407.677.5600
Clearwater	2640 Gulf to Bay Boulevard
	813.799.1808
Fort Lauderdale	665 NW 62nd Street
	305.771.2800
Fort Myers	12984 Cleveland Avenue
	941.433.1441
Gainesville	3208 SW Archer Avenue
	904.373.2800
Hallandale	602 East Hallandale Beach. Boulevard
	305.458.0070
Hollywood	5181 Sheridan Street
	954.961.8332
Jacksonville	8532 Baymeadows Road
	904.731.3075
Jacksonville	8440 Blanding Boulevard
	904.771.6624
Jacksonville	9245 Atlantic Boulevard
	904.724.0991
Lakeland	3901 North 98th Street
	941.853.9492
Lakeland	3621 South Florida Avenue
	941.646.8550
Melbourne	900 South Apollo Boulevard
	407.727.1180
Miami	13603 South Dixie Highway
	305.378.8618
Miami	11460 North Kendall Drive
	305.271.7863

Miami Springs	3449 LeJeune Road 305.871.4282
North Miami Beach	940 NE 163rd Street 305.948.6733
Ocala	3155 Silver Springs Boulevard 904.351.3910
Orlando	6324 International Drive 407.351.4435
Orlando	7630 South Orange Blossom Trail 407.851.1266
Orlando	6109 Westwood Boulevard 407.352.5657
Orlando	4250 East Colonial Drive 407.896.6516
Ormand Beach	890 South Atlantic Avenue 904.673.3691
Palm Beach Gardens	4050 PGA Boulevard 407.694.1723
Pensacola	7253 Plantation Road 904.474.0668
Sarasota	1277 South Tamiami Trail 941.953.9742
St. Petersburg	4625 Gulf Boulevard 813.367.4521
St. Petersburg	9900 4th Street North 813.576.7735
St. Petersburg	2126 Tyrone Boulevard North 813.343.1075
Sunrise	3499 North University Drive 305.748.3991
Tallahassee	830 East Lafayette Street 904.878.4405
Tampa	2520 North Dale Mabry Highway 813.872.7566
Tampa	13262 North Dale Mabry Highway 813.872.9668
Tampa	2206 East Fowler Avenue 813.977.3506

| West Palm Beach | 2070 Palm Beach Lakes Boulevard |
| | 407.689.5010 |

Georgia

Athens	140 Alps Road
	706.543.5960
Atlanta	3274 Northlake Boulevard
	404.493.1593
Atlanta	3400 Woodale Drive NE
	404.262.7142
College Park	2144 Sullivan Road
	770.762.8400
Macon	2460 Riverside Drive
	912.742.5116
Morrow	1213 Morrow Industrial Boulevard
	770.961.0399
Norcross	5395 Jimmy Carter Boulevard
	770.449.7219
Savannah	6705 Abercorn Street
	912.355.0478

Illinois

Calumet City	1250 Torrence Avenue
	708.868.6809
Chicago	225 North Michigan Avenue
	312.938.9080
Chicago	150 South Michigan Avenue
	312.427.0577
Chicago	8420 West Byrn Mawr Avenue
	312.380.1010
Chicago	555 West Madison Street
	312.902.2500
Chicago Ridge	6401 West 95th Street
	708.499.6808
Niles	8480 Golf Road
	708.965.4644
Normal	115 Veterans Parkway
	309.454.5577

Oakbrook Terrace	17 West 460 22nd Street
	630.832.5611
Schaumburg	1770 East Higgins Road
	847.517.7785
Woodridge	1001 East 75th Street
	708.985.5003

Iowa

Clear Lake	Highway 18 & I–35
	515.357.2366
Rock Falls	2105 1st Ave
	815.626.5500

Kansas

Overland Park	9520 Metcalf Avenue
	913.341.0103
Topeka	3251 South Topeka Boulevard
	913.266.6660
Wichita	111 South Rock Road
	316.681.3255

LOUISIANA

Baton Rouge	9770 Cortana Place
	504.924.3659
Bossier City	2950 East Texas Street, Ste 108
	318.752.5700
Kenner	2701 Veterans Memorial Boulevard
	504.468.1072
Lafayette	3511 Ambassador Caffery Parkway
	318.981.5534
Metairie	3434 Veterans Memorial Boulevard
	504.888.0664
New Orleans	3010 Holiday Drive
	504.394.2805

Maryland

Baltimore	34 Market Place
	410.837.0553
Baltimore	6975 Security Boulevard
	944.994.1880
Columbia	5585 Sterrett Place
	410.740.4448
Greenbelt	6002 Greenbelt Road
	301.982.9780
Laurel	14180 Baltimore Avenue
	301.776.4412
Rockville	12276 Rockville Pike
	301.770.2594

Massachusetts

Boston	8 Park Plaza
	617.227.3754
Framingham	155 Worcester Road
	508.879.3937
Peabody	71 Newbury Street
	508.535.2932

Michigan

Ann Arbor	575 Briarwood Circle
	313.996.0996
Bloomfield Hills	2555 Woodward Avenue
	810.334.9810
Flint	2372 Austins Parkway
	810.238.4033
Okemos	2085 West Grand River Avenue
	517.349.2321
Plymouth	40441 Ann Arbor Road
	313.459.8907
Madison Heights	32787 Stephenson Highway
	810.583.9835

Southfield	28555 Northwestern Highway
	810.356.0292
Warren	30700 Van Dyke Avenue
	810.573.8230

Minnesota

Bloomington*	1800 West 80th Street
	612.881.0013
St. Louis Park*	6475 Wayzata Boulevard
	612.593.5024

Mississippi

Jackson	4525 Interstate Highway. 55 North
	601.362.8375

Missouri

Kansas City	5540 East Bannister Road
	816.966.8549

Nevada

Stateline*	Highway 50
	702.588.5977

New Jersey

Englewood	412 South Van Brunt Street
	201.569.9797
Fairfield	646 Route 46 East
	201.882.0162
Florham Park	119 Columbia Turnpike
	201.822.7930
Metuchen	65 US Highway 1
	908.548.5557
Morristown	1 Speedwell Avenue
	201.538.9855

Mt. Laurel	1109 Route 73
	609.235.4190
New Brunswick	Route 1 & Route 18
	908.846.8700
North Brunswick	2241 Route 1 South
	908.297.8200
Ocean Township	1912 State Route 35
	908.531.2999
Parsippany	1735 US Route 46
	201.335.6880
Plainfield	4901 Stelton Road
	908.769.0380
Ramsey	66 Route 17 North
	201.934.9390
Saddlebrook	405 North Midland Avenue
	201.794.0213
Springfield	272 Route 22
	201.564.6016

New Mexico

Albuquerque	2105 B. Louisiana Boulevard
	505.883.1665
Albuquerque	6321 San Mateo Boulevard NE
	505.881.4262

New York

Amherst	4060 Maple Road
	716.833.3550
Amherst	7516 Transit Road
	716.632.5049
Brentwood	300 Motor Parkway
	516.434.7890
Garden City	711 Stewart Avenue
	516.222.1305
Great Neck	26 Great Neck Road
	516.829.8120
New City	258 South Main Street
	914.638.9303

North Babylon	1112 Deer Park Avenue
	516.254.0211
Syracuse	2841 Erie Boulevard East
	315.446.7575

North Carolina

Charlotte	4717 Sharon Road
	704.366.0942
Fayetteville	225 North McPherson Church Road
	910.864.5558
Greensboro	3035 High Point Road
	910.299.4784
Raleigh	4128 Six Forks Road
	919.782.5468
Wilmington	318 South College Boulevard
	910.791.0012
Winston Salem	7838 North Point Boulevard
	910.759.0920

Ohio

Cincinnati	4550 Glendale Milford Road
	513.733.9666
Cincinnati	9035 Fields-Ertel Road
	513.697.8100
Dayton	7260 Miller Lane
	937.264.1333
Springdale	12140 Springfield Pike
	513.671.2112

Oklahoma

Oklahoma City	13593 North May Avenue
	405.752.7600
Oklahoma City	4300 West I-40 Service Road
	405.946.0747

| Tulsa | 7030 South Zurich Avenue |
| | 918.492.6202 |

Pennsylvania

King of Prussia	160 North Gulph Road
	610.337.0633
Montgomeryville	678 Bethlehem Pike
	215.412.7777
Philadelphia	2231 Cottman Avenue
	215.722.1907
Philadelphia	11000 Roosevelt Boulevard
	215.677.4667
Springfield	720 Baltimore Pike
	215.328.0612
Wayne	1 Devon Square, Lancaster Pike
	610.964.1100
Willow Grove	2402 Easton Road
	215.674.8383

Tennessee

Chattannooga	5621 Brainerd Road
	615.899.5650
Johnson City	2280 North Roan Street
	615.282.8552
Memphis	5336 Poplar Avenue
	901.685.2088
Nashville	975 Murfreesboro Road
	615.361.3996

Texas

Amarillo	3401 I–40 West
	806.358.7409
Arlington	721 North Watson Road
	817.640.6088
Arlington	4000 South Cooper Street
	817.467.3363
Austin	7604 I–35 North
	512.451.7953

Austin	301 Barton Springs Road
	512.472.7902
Beaumont	325 I–10 North
	409.833.2648
Bedford	2101 West Airport Freeway
	817.354.7030
College Station	1505 A Texas Avenue South
	409.696.9066
Dallas	12505 East Northwest Highway
	972.270.9060
Dallas	2410 Walnut Hill Lane
	214.350.3127
Dallas	8139 Park Lane
	214.696.2080
Dallas	5260 Belt Line Road
	972.233.2107
Dallas	13350 Dallas Parkway, Dallas Galleria
	972.385.9988
Dallas	4345 West Camp Wisdom Road
	972.296.0422
Dallas	3858 West Northwest Highway
	972.358.2432
El Paso	10497 Gateway Boulevard West
	915.592.7200
Friendswood	1330 West Bay Area Boulevard
	713.480.2695
Fort Worth	4833 S Hulen Street
	817.294.1021
Fort Worth	8250 Bedford Euless Road
	817.498.6620
Fort Worth	6540 Camp Bowie Boulevard
	817.732.6022
Fort Worth	5751 Bridge Street
	817.457.1966
Houston	1200 McKinney Street, Suite 475
	713.654.9400
Houston	9811 Bissonnet Street
	713.774.6033
Houston	5015 Westheimer Road
	713.621.3921

Houston	222 North Belt 281.820.4776
Houston	2700 South Loop West 713.660.7380
Houston	6501 Southwest Freeway 713.778.1973
Houston	4505 FM 1960 West 713.893.7011
Houston	7143 Gulf Freeway 713.644.9691
Houston	12008 East Freeway 713.453.4008
Houston	10811 Westheimer Road 713.789.1525
Houston	211 West FM 1960 713.444.1433
Houston	1030 West Belt Drive North 713.827.0720
Houston	10690 Northwest Freeway 713.957.3312
Houston	3963 Kirby Drive 713.524.5884
Humble	140 FM 1960 East Bypass 281.446.4646
Irving	122 East John Carpenter Freeway 214.541.0333
Irving	4300 West Airport Freeway 972.986.5444
Lewisville	2290 South Stemmons Freeway 972.315.6206
Midland	4517 North Midkiff Road 915.697.3237
Plano	1910 North Central Expressway 972.424.4519
Plano	4900 West Park Boulevard 972.964.1036
San Antonio	9837 I–10 West 210.690.6007
San Antonio	7439 San Pedro Avenue 210.342.6087

Tyler	3304 Troup Highway
	903.592.6771
Wichita Falls	4521 Kemp Boulevard
	214.692.8844

Virginia

Alexandria	2 South Whiting Street
	703.370.7511
Fairfax	11778 Upper Fair Oaks Mall
	703.691.2208
Falls Church	6290 Arlington Boulevard
	703.237.6288
Hampton	2092 Coliseum Drive
	804.838.9261
Norfolk	5741 East Virginia Beach Boulevard
	804.461.0661
Springfield	6632 Springfield Mall
	703.922.6004
Richmond	8000 West Broad Street
	804.270.3043
Vienna	8219 Leesburg Pike
	703.556.9417
Virginia Beach	757 Lynhaven Parkway
	804.463.7100

West Virginia

Charleston	1119 Charleston Town Center
	304.343.4281

Under construction

Texarkana, AK	420 Realtor Avenue
Kingsland, GA	930 Highway 40
Clinton T'ship, MI	37015 Gratiot Avenue
Mt Pleasant, MI	2400 South Mission Street

Chapter
6
Beer style guide

Three beers that changed the industry

PORTER, PALE ALE, and Pilsner, each, from different locations, changed the course of beer's history. The first two are British, Porter from London, Pale Ale initially from London, but muscled out by brewers at Burton upon Trent, with which it is now identified. The third is Czech, the eponymous Pilsner from Plzen in the province of Bohemia.

Before I describe each beer style in the guide, let us first examine these three important beers in turn and see why each is so.

Porter

PORTER IS THE beer style that led directly to the growth of commercial brewing in London in the 1700s. Before then, most brewing was done by the pubs themselves. Because Porter has a long maturing process, much longer than pub-brewers could afford to match, they gradually lost ground to the newly-formed commercial brewers. Porter was so popular that controlling Porter production led to dominance of the brewing market. This was in London where Porter was popular, but in the countryside it was a different story where regular ales were still preferred. It wasn't until efficient cooling systems were developed that the inhibition warm weather had on ale brewing was lifted, thus allowing commercial brewers outside London to move into the market of providing quality beer during those months. Gradually commercial brewers improved their techniques and equipment until, finally, they were able to provide beer pub-brewers could not match in price, consistency and quality. Pub-brewers gave up.

In the late 1800s there was a middle-class revolt against Porter, and the shift was on to Pale Ales. Lighter-colored ale was in, Porter was out. It went into decline and, by the 1914–18 war, it had all but disappeared.

Today Porter is having a revival on both sides of the Atlantic. It's growth has been triggered by growing interest by the drinking public in darker specialty beers. Most Porters are brewed by micro-breweries, such as Sierra Nevada, and brew-pubs. One can not be sure if these are in the same mold as original Porters because present-day brewers are working from very old recipes, the original Porter yeasts have been lost, and the brown malts that used to go into Porter are no longer made. Sad but true.

Pale Ale

Dark ale to the right of them. Dark ale to the left of them. Dark ale in front of them. In to the Valley of Darkness rode the brave 600. It was Pale Ale Brigade that lead the first charge against dark ale. As with any conflict, it is not necessarily the first action that brings about change. However, it does initiate the process.

Until the development of manufacturing techniques that permitted both the kilning of pale malt and the mass production of glass-ware, all beer was dark. Some writers have described all early dark beer as murky, with all sorts of vile particles suspended in it, but this is surely an exaggeration, at the least, or the careless use of anecdotal material to condemn the lot.

The development of inexpensive, readily available glassware allowed publicans to present beer in a more attractive way than with the previously-used solid drinking vessels. British class structure also led to Pale Ale's rise to prominence over dark beer. The middle and upper classes sought to distinguish themselves from the working class who stuck with dark beer.

Traditionally, strong India Pale Ale was brewed for British Empire troops stationed in India, from the 18th century until 1945, when India gained independence. It was originally formulated by Mark Hodgson, a London brewer, sometime between 1790 and 1800. His IPA enabled him to dominate the export market to India up to about 1830. He was exporting 9,000 barrels per year by 1807 and this rose to 41,000 barrels per year by 1817.

Meanwhile, Burton brewers saw their Baltic export market collapse due to Napolean Bonaparte's conquest of that area. Britain and France were at war. The brewers sought new markets. As a result, Allsopp and Bass began brewing India Pale Ale, and within a short time were mounting a challenge to Mr. Hodgson, their rival.

The Burton IPA variant was a pale, sparkling ale. It was heavily hopped and highly-conditioned. The beer had to be strong and hoppy to survive the long sea-journey there, which could take as long as six months under sail. Aesthetic reasons also were influential in deciding on its pale color.

Pale Ale remains the most-popular ale to this day.

Pilsner

THE PREDOMINANT STYLE throughout the world (except in Great Britain) only developed in 1842. Three years earlier, in 1839, residents of Pilsen, in what is now the Czech Republic, asked permission to build their own brewery because they were unhappy with the ales then on offer. As luck would have it, the water in the area, being very hard, was excellent for brewing pale lagers. Approximately 5.5 miles of under ground cellars were cut into the sandstone. They provided a perfect temperature for lagering beer. Production quickly increased as demand from afar spurred export to Berlin, London, München, Paris and Wien. By the 1870s, Pilsner was famous throughout Europe. Urquell was added to the name to show its original source, after other European brewers began imitating the style. Major variations developed in München, Wien, and Dortmund.

Simultaneously, German-speaking brewers migrating to North America brought the style with them. Obviously, they used North American grown barley and other grains, which imparted somewhat different characteristics to their beers. Millions of fellow immigrants were their built-in market. Within 50 years, light-colored lager had dealt a knockout blow to ale, which is just now staggering back to its feet. Evidence of lager's romp over ale lies in the fact that virtually all North American breweriana in existence from the mid 1800s onward are from German- not British-named breweries. The situation remains the same today.

In an era when beer was shipped rather slowly in casks and kegs, lager enjoyed an overlooked advantage (with rare exception) over ale. It traveled better, meaning it could be shipped greater distances and still maintained its drinkability. This allowed lager brewers to expand their market areas to continental magnitude, whereas ale brewers remained, in the main, local. The first national breweries that operated on such a scale were North American.

However, it must be said that with scientific and technical advancements, modern packaging (bottles, cans, and stainless steel kegs), and fast transport, lager no longer enjoys the advantage of having better traveling legs.

Also, as with Pale Ale, light-colored lagers look more appealing in glass. Pilsner has been called "Champagne with a head." With one glance it is obvious to see why.

Pilsner beer, and the brewing revolution it helped start, supplanted ale everywhere in the world except Britain. Considering that there was only ale-brewing for millennia, it is remarkable that in less than one hundred years, the beer-drinking tastes of the human race changed so dramatically.

Porter lead to the establishment of large commercial breweries in Great Britain. Pale Ale broke dark beer's reign, and led to increased commerce in beer throughout the British Empire and beyond and, within 100 years, Pilsner almost completely replaced ale as the most preferred beer round the world, with Great Britain being the sole exception.

A closer look at beer styles

In this section I will describe all current styles, a few traditional ones, and the odd extinct style. Description of each have been drawn from various sources, and from personal research. Original Gravity is given (where available) so one can compare it to alcohol content. The comparison gives some indication of how attenuated the beer is. Attenuation is an indicator of how much residual malt sweetness there might be in the beer, and, too, body.

KEY MEASUREMENTS	
ABV	ALCOHOL BY VOLUME
ABW	ALCOHOL BY WEIGHT
OG	ORIGINAL GRAVITY
IBUS	INTERNATIONAL BITTERING UNITS

Alcohol content will, in every instance, be percent by volume (instead of by weight, which is more difficult to figure) and displayed, as an example, 4.5% ABV. Hop bittering units are expressed in International Bittering Units (IBUS). The greater the number, the more hop bitterness is in the beer. Bear in mind the taste threshold for hop bitterness is 8–12 IBUS.

Color ranges are given in both SRM (Standard Reference Method) and EBC (European Brewery Convention) scales.

As a reference, below is the SRM color scale.

Color	SRM	Color	SRM
Water	0	Light amber	5.5–10.0
Light straw	1.0–2.5	Pale amber	10–18
Pale straw	2.5–3.5	Dark amber or copper	18–26
Dark straw	3.5–5.5		
Deep copper or brown	26–40	Black	>40

A brief reminder: the determining factor that traditionally places a particular beer in one category or the other is the yeast type used. While there are many strains of yeast, they are divided into top-fermenting and bottom-fermenting types. Top-fermenting yeasts are ale yeasts. Bottom-fermenting yeasts are lager yeasts. To keep which is which straight in mind, think of top as above and bottom as lower. The first letter of above and ale match; the first letter of lower and lager match.

Another distinguishing characteristic between ale and lager yeast is the temperature at which they are active. Ale yeasts ferment best at temperatures above of 15-25°C (59-77°F), while lager yeasts continue to work down to about 34°F (1°C). It is easy to guess what type beer is in the barrels when one examines photographs of cold-looking beer storage cellars.

There are three beer styles that are hybrids, two of which are genuinely American. Developed in the late 19th century, they use lager yeast (normally), but are fermented at ale temperatures then lagered at cold temperatures. This is a style that is tricky to brew because lager yeasts impart off-flavors when fermented at warm temperatures, a problem home-brewers know all-to-well. It is also the reason why they don't often attempt lager brewing unless they have a beer-dedicated refrigerator or live in Northern regions where they can brew lagers during winter.

There are on-going debates about styles among brewers, beer judges, and others in the industry, notably beer writers. The debate has centered round a core of issues (questions, really): how loose or tight should style parameters be? Should they be flexible or rigid? How to define styles? Should brewers be called to task if they label a brand a certain style when it certainly is not?–or should we even care? Are there too many style designations, and if so how could they be pared? Should exceptions be made for a single brand that is unique–give it its own style designation, or should it be tossed into the closest-appropriate one?

For some, simply to determine if a beer drinks well (or not) is enough. Notice I did not mention the taste of the beer. There is a difference between drinking beer (as to quench a thirst) and tasting beer (to enjoy it). Others want to learn everything they can about beer.

It is human nature to categorize everything. It is that upon which science is built. Every species, every element, every atom and particle in this universe that has been discovered has been studied and described and categorized. It is the way of man.

Why should it be any different when it comes to beer? It shouldn't, but there are practical limits beyond which categorization becomes pedantic. It is not the purpose of this book to delve into these discussions, but to illustrate but a single point: imagine two brewers who set out to brew the same beer—which style isn't important. They use the exact same recipe: the amounts of the same variety hops; they boil the wort for the same length of time; they use the same yeast strain; and they use the same amounts of pale malt, but with this difference—they use different suppliers. One's barley is malted to a slightly darker color than that of the other maltster. This results in a perceptibly, but only slightly, darker beer that tastes just a wee bit sweeter. Should both still be classified in the same style? Of course. What if, instead of using the darker grain, that brewer used a different hop? One that gave the beer a more floral aroma? The two would probably still be grouped together. But what if the different hops made that beer much more hoppy to the palate, as is the difference between a Continental Light Lager and a Continental Pilsner? Here the two have to be separated.

Some differences between styles are subtle and narrow, and others are oceans apart. There has to be some variation within a style, but the variation cannot be called a new style unless it is perceived as too different or too changed. Stout developed from Porter. It was at first called Stout Porter, meaning strong Porter. Then roasted unmalted barley was introduced into the recipe, which changed the taste somewhat (and darkened the color still further). The changes in Porter were enough that Stout came to be recognized as a style unto itself. The two coexisted for a while, then Porter went down the road to oblivion while Stout prospered. Now, Porter is back, but trying to regain its identity. It is still defining itself, or, more accurately, the brewers are.

The Confederation of Belgian Brewers appears to consider almost every brand to be a unique style, and I wouldn't want to put ourselves through the enormous effort to learn, define and profile each of those styles. That is a bit much.

As a direct result of the craft beer movement, nearly all European beer styles are now being brewed in North American using New World ingredients and different yeast. The result are beers that taste different than the European originals, though the basic recipes are the same. Therefore, I have created new designations for many North American-brewed styles.

New styles will develop. It is bound to happen as more curious people who aren't afraid to experiment take up the craft. Perhaps the next new style will be the result of an accidental discovery, or perhaps the result of a carefully thought out effort. I do not care how it comes about, just as long as the result is delicious, and made from quality ingredients. I encourage readers to seek and try beers of the different styles: the written word seldom does justice to actual experience.

Beer style guide

Ale

Top-fermented beer

Ale Beer Styles

Belgian Aged Beers:
- Old Brown
- Old Red
- Old Pale

Holy Beers:
- Trappiste
- Abbey

Pale & Amber Ales:
- Best Bitter or Special Bitter
- Extra Special Bitter
- Bitter (Amber & Red)
- Irish Ale
- Scottish Ales
- Speciaal
- Pale Ale
- Golden Ale & Canadian Ale
- India Pale Ale (IPA)

Strong Ales:
- Strong Golden
- Old Ale
- Barleywine
- Dubbel and Trippel
- Belgium
- Extra Strong Ale
- Scotch Ale
- Bière de Garde

Dark Ales:
- Mild
- Brown Ale
- Porter/Entire

Stouts:
- Dry Stout
- Sweet Stout
- Oatmeal Stout
- Double Stout
- Imperial Stout

Seasonal Ales:
- Christmas Ale/Winter Warmers
- Bière de Noel
- Saison
- Bière de Mars

Wheat Beers:
- Berliner Weisse
- Weisse
- Grätzerbier
- Weizen-Weissbier
- Dunkel Weizenbier
- Steinweizen
- Weizenbock
- Weizen Doppelbock
- Witbier or Bière Blanche
- Wheat Beer

Wild Yeast Beers:
- Faro
- Gueuze
- Lambic Doux
- Lambic Blanche Wit

Other Ales:
- Tafelbier - Bière de Table
- Grand Cru and Cuvée
- Dampfbier
- Steinbier

Fruit Beers:
- Kriek (Cherry) Lambic
- Frambozen (Raspberry) Lambic
- Peche (Peach) Lambic
- Kriek (Cherry) Gueuze
- Frambozen (Raspberry) Gueuze
- Old Driek (Old Cherry)
- Old Frambozen (Old Raspberry)

Spiced Beers

Native Beers

Ale-Lager Hybrids:
- Pils Ale
- Altbier
- Kölsch

Belgian aged beers

Oud Bruin or Old Brown–Belgian Brown Ale

These are sometimes called *zuur* (sour) beers. Bottle-conditioned, the style originated in the East Flanders region of Belgium, and are an interesting lot. They are loved or hated with equal passion because of their distinctly sour taste and, often, aroma. This is by design, not the result of something gone very wrong during the fermenting or lagering stage–though originally it was.

Color ranges from red to brown to almost black. Body is light to medium. Aromas–there can be many, and are induced from the bacteria, micro-organisms and yeasts: malty and sweet, acidic, port and sherry wine-like, floral and fruity. Oud Bruins will not have a hoppy aroma or flavor. Almost all Belgian beer styles are very lightly hopped. Two and three year old hops are often used because their aromatic properties have evaporated, though their bittering and preservative ones remain. Sazz, Goldings and Styrian hops which are low-bittering, but not overly aromatic are preferred. On the palate expect slight vinegar or lactic sourness, and spicy notes well-blended with a lovely malt base. Some brands exhibit some diacetyl and roast malt notes as well.

Unlike their British cousins, Belgian Brown Ales often are aged a long time after they come out of the finishing tanks. In the case of Liefman's Goudenband, it has 3–12 month's bottle-maturation. If it is kept cool (but not refrigerated) and in a dark place, it will improve with age and reach its peak in, say, two years.

Color 12–18SRM, 30–50EBC; bitterness 15–25IBUS; alcohol content 4.8–5.2% ABV.

Old Red–Sour beer–Belgium

This Belgian style is one of the finest and most exquisite beers in the world. It is exemplified by Rodenbach's Belgian Red Ale and Grand Cru. Both are fermented at least 18 months in enormous uncoated wood tanks that stand some 20 feet high. The flavors imparted by the wood add much character to the beer.

Standard Rodenbach Red is a blend of two beers. The first is a 1052OG that is aged for at least 18 months. The second is five to six weeks old with 1046OG. The result is 5.2% ABV.

This red-brown beer is similar to Burgundy in color. Body is thin, but with substance. Sourness and fruit are clearly evident in the nose. There are clear notes of Madeira, oak, and fruit on the palate. The finish is long, bitter, and sour.

Rodenbach Red Ale is brewed using four malts (80%), one pale summer malt, two- and six-row winter malts and Vienna crystal malt, which imparts the red cast to the beer, and maize grits (20%). Belgian-grown Brewers Gold and some Kent Goldings hops are used. Five different yeasts strains are used, plus any lactobacillus that have taken up residence in the oak tuns. These impart the unique freshness and sourness to this world-class beer. Unlike its Brown brother, this style is pasteurized.

Rodenbach's similar Grand Cru has an alcohol content of 1064OG, 6.6% ABV; bitterness is 14EBUS; color is 5.5SRM, 60EBC.

Taste is sweet and sour at the same time. There are strong caramel notes, and tannins from the wood are clearly evident, along with sourness.

Old Pale–Belgium

This style is similar to Old Brown. The difference is that Old Pale uses much lighter malts thereby resulting in a paler-colored beer. Alcohol content and bitterness are also similar to Old Brown.

Holy Beers

Trappiste & Abbey Ale–Belgium

Trappiste

There are five Trappist monasteries in Belgium and one in the Netherlands that can, by law, use the word "Trappiste" in their beer descriptions.

Trappiste beers are usually strong, from 6–10% ABV, and use candy sugar (glucose chips or dextrose) in their formulation. They are always bottle-conditioned, and their color ranges from bronze to deep brown. Following ancient traditions some brands get flavored and/or scented with spices such as coriander, cumin and ginger.

These beers are really a subset of the category, though each is distinctive of the others due to the various yeast strains and bacteria (there are usually several in each beer). In one aspect of their brewing process, these are closest to beer as it was originally made thousands of years ago: once the wort has been boiled, the beer is cooled and left exposed to the air until it picks up airborne yeasts and bacteria until fermentation begins.

Abbey

The English word *abbey* (Flemish: *abdij;* French: *abbaye;* German: *abtei*) should be used to describe any beer brewed in a Trappist style, but not at one of the six monasteries.

Too often the use of the word Abbey on beer labels has been misused by some commercial brewers to create a false status to their brands. This is not always the case. There are several Abbey beers that are delicious.

Pale & Amber Ales

Bitter–England

To drink properly cask-conditioned and dispensed Bitter and its cousins Best Bitter and Extra Special Bitter, is an experience well worth the journey to Britain, where it is a national treasure to those who care about such things. Unlike many other styles,which are very narrowly defined, the delight of Bitter is its breadth and depth of color, aromas, bouquet, body, palate and finish.

In England, cask Bitter is the draft equivalent of Pale Ale. As the name implies, they are well-hopped with medium bitterness. Color ranges from gold to deep copper. The body is light to medium. Some acidity in the finish, as well as residual malt sweetness, is to be expected. Ordinary Bitter has low alcohol range, and carbonation is low to medium.

The three bitter styles account for about 80% of draft beer sales in Britain.

Color 8–12SRM, 16–30EBC; bitterness 20–35IBUS; alcohol content 1033–400G, 3.5–4.0% ABV.

Best or Special Bitter–England

Special Bitter is a mid-octane, more robust Bitter with 1038–10450G, 4.0–4.8% ABV. Bitterness 28–46IBUS; color 12–14SRM, 30–35EBC. They tend to be medium-bodied, hoppy and dry, with medium residual malt sweetness.

Extra Special Bitter–England

These are high-octane–1046–560G, 4.8–5.8% ABV, about double the strength of standard Mild. Bitterness is 30–55IBUS; color is 12–14SRM, 30–35EBC. They are also highly attenuated, giving more alcohol than their original gravities would suggest.

Compared to Bitter and Best Bitter, Extra Special Bitter is maltier, has more body and bitterness, but more residual malt sweetness.

Bitter (Amber & Red Ale)–North America craft

This is the North American version of British Bitter. Many North American brewers are afraid to name their beer "Bitter" because the term is not understood by many people in the States. Instead, they've settled on Amber or Red Ale as a safe alternative.

North American grown hops and malts are expected to be used here, but that is not rigid. Many brewers use British hops, especially Goldings varieties, and malts, but call the result Amber Ale.

Color ranges from light copper to light brown. Hop rates are medium to high in nose, bitterness and palate. Malt should be medium to high to balance the hop bitterness, and low to medium rates of caramel are expected, too. Body is medium. Fruity ester notes in the nose and palate are desirable.

Color 11–18SRM, 10–25EBC; 4.5–5.5% ABV, 1044–56OG; bitterness 20–40IBUS.

Extra Special Bitter–North America craft

This is an emerging style in North America, perhaps because its specifications, especially alcohol content, better suits North American preferences. Americans prefer their beer with about 1.0–1.5% ABV above what British drinkers like. Another reason could be the cachet Fullers has given the style with their tremendous ESB, which has become a popular import.

Specifications should be about the same as its British cousin, but with alcohol content upper limit a little higher, at, say 6.0% ABV, and with North American ingredients, which alter the aroma and taste characteristics.

Irish Ale–Ireland

This variation of Pale Ale is similar to, but lighter and paler than Scottish ale. The use of caramel malt gives it its copper-red color.

This style appears to have died out in Ireland in 1956 when G H Lett, the brewer, of Enniscorthy, County Wexford ceased production, and licensed its Ruby Ale to Pelforth, the French brewing concern. Later, Coors of North America acquired it, where it is known as Killian's Irish Red. Coors brews this beer as a lager, so it cannot be considered here.

The style seems to be undergoing a rebirth in North America where brew-pubs and micro-breweries are searching for styles to brew to separate themselves from their competitors.

Perhaps North American versions should be more properly classified as North American Amber Ales, and this style left to the appropriate genuine Irish-brewed ales.

Color 8–25SRM; bitterness 18–32IBUS; alcohol content 1044–48OG, 3.7–5.0% ABV.

Scottish Ales-Scotland

Scottish ales are noticeably different from those brewed in England. Because hops are not native north of Hadrian's Wall, Scots brewers came rather late to using it. When they did, they tended to use much less of it than their southern neighbors. Hence, a less bitter, but sweeter beer compared with English ales.

They are brewed in three styles: Light, Heavy, and Export. Light is comparable to English Mild. Heavy, in name only, is similar to Ordinary Bitter, and Export is close to Special Bitter.

The modern parameters for the three are as follows:

Light: color 8–17SRM; bitterness 9–20IBUS; 1035–1040OG, 2.8–3.5% ABV.

Heavy: color 10–19SRM; bitterness 15–20IBUS; alcohol content 1035–40OG, 3.5–4.0% ABV.

Export: color 10–19SRM; bitterness 15–20IBUS; alcohol content 1040–50OG, 4.0–5.0% ABV.

Speciaal (Special)–Belgium

This style, in Belgium, has different parameters than the British one of the same name. The word *Speciaal* on the bottle label indicates the weakest pale ale on a brewery's list. This is confusing to an unknowing drinker, as one would think it indicative of a superior, not inferior, brand.

Pale Ale–England, traditional

The 1914–18 war, and the taxman contributed to the decline of traditional British ales. The government, keen to keep war-effort workers sober and in the factories, clamped down on barley malt (and pub opening hours). As a result, brewers were forced to produce weaker beer. Traditional high alcohol content styles never recovered. The rise in excise on alcohol content had a similar compounding effect. To keep the price of a pint at a reasonable level, brewers had to make weaker beer. This effect has continued. As recently as 1995, many British brewers were again lowering the alcohol content of their beers due to excise pressures. The result is beer that would have been, in pre-war times, thought of as merely table beer of 5.0% ABV, or less.

A typical 1900 English Pale Ale had a 1057OG, and 76IBUs, the latter about double today's hopping rate. Prior to 1900, Pale Ales were even stronger.

Pale Ale–England

This is one of the classic beer styles in the world. It may be considered the ale that is matched opposite Pilsner. Pale Ale has a color range from golden amber to copper, and is brewed with pale malts and very hard water.

Pale, in this usage, does not mean its obvious definition but, rather, pale in comparison to Brown Ale, Porter, and Stout. They have low to moderate alcohol content. Pale Ale is, often, not as highly attenuated as is Bitter, so it tends to be a bit heavier than the latter.

Bullion, Fuggles, Goldings, and Target hops are most frequently used, though others are used.

Color 8–12SRM, 16–30EBC; bitterness 19–45IBUS; alcohol content 1035–56OG, 3.4–5.5% ABV.

One must note there is a distinction between Pale Ales as a broad classification of ales and Pale Ale as a bottled beer name. The term Pale Ale is often used by brewers to label their best bitters, especially if they are bottled.

Pale Ale–Belgium

The people of Belgian and Britain have had a long historical association. Belgian tribesmen gave Julius Caesar intelligence on the Britons before the Romans invaded the island. In 1816, Wellington, the Iron Duke, with Prussian reinforcements, defeated Napoleon, the scourge of Europe, at Waterloo, some 18 kilometers south of Brussels. Both the 1914–18 and the 1939–45 wars saw heavy British involvement in Belgium. This long tie led to the popularity of British and Scottish ales in Belgium.

Stylistically, Belgian Pale Ale is more similar to Scottish Ale, with lower hop usage than employed by English brewers. However, the use of different hops and Belgian yeasts impart some dissimilar notes, particularly fruity esters in low to moderate amounts in both aroma and on the palate. Color should be deep golden (never light-gold) to deep amber. Hops should be low, but noticeable in the aroma, over soft malt notes, and on the palate. Body should be light to medium

Color 3.5–12SRM, 8–39EBC; bitterness is 19–55IBUS; Alcohol content 4.0–6.0% ABV; 1040–1060OG.

Pale Ale–North America-craft

Here is a style that North American craft brewers have clearly out-shown their British colleagues. At a gathering of beer critics and experts in England to discuss, compare, taste, and judge British and North American Pale Ales, the North American brands ran away from the field.

Many North American brewers use English barley, but strong Pacific North-west copper hops, and Cascade hops in the finish, which imparts lovely grapefruit notes in the aroma and the palate. Too, Chico, or similar standard "American" ale yeasts are employed. The combinations work exceedingly well.

Color is golden to almost medium copper. American-grown hops are required. They impart strong bitterness, readily apparent in the aroma. Body should be medium.

Color 4–11SRM, 10–25EBC; bitterness 20–40IBUS; alcohol content 1044–10560G, 4.5–5.5% ABV.

Golden Ale & Canadian Ale–North America

Not to be confused with the Cream Ale, the Ale-Lager hybrid, this style can be compared closely with American Lager, in that both are crisp, dry on the palate, and are extremely light-colored. They are a version of North American Pale Ale.

A floral hop aroma should be low but noticeable, and the body should be light. Fruity notes in the aroma and on the palate, while perceived, should not predominate.

Color 3–10SRM, 7–20EBC; bitterness 15–30IBUS; alcohol content 1045–560G, 4.0–5.0% ABV.

India Pale Ale (IPA)–England, traditional

The first IPAS might have been brewed to 1070–900G, with bitterness of 150IBUS. Those are staggering numbers, by today's standards. Fuggle and Kent Golding hops would have been used, both in copper and as dry hops in the cask to add extra flavor and aroma.

The peak of the export trade for IPAS was the 1880s. By then, faster sailing ships and steamers considerably shortened sailing time from Britain to India. This allowed brewers to reduce the strength and bitterness. The specifications at that time were 1060–70G, 7.0–8.4% ABV; bitterness 55–70IBUS; color 12–18SRM. Quite a fall in 100 years, but still higher and darker than today's standards.

India Pale Ale (IPA)–England

A case could be made by some that modern British IPA, can't hold a candle to Traditional IPA in both alcohol content and character.

Even the color has considerably lightened. In some instances, it is nearly as light as Blonde or Golden Ales. Some brewers try to capitalize on the recognition of the term IPA, and label their beers as such, when in reality they are simply a Bitter or Pale Ale.

IPAS should be brewed with 'Burtonized' water, meaning it is either naturally very hard with high mineral content, or it should be treated at the brewery to make it so. Hop rates should be high, so hop aromas should be strong to very strong, and bitterness should be intense on the palate. Body should be medium, with plenty of malt to balance the intense hop bitterness. Fruity ester notes should be moderate to very strong in both aroma and palate.

Color 8–14SRM, 16–30EBU; bitterness 40–60IBUS; alcohol content 1050–10700G; 5.0–7.5% ABV;

India Pale Ale–North America craft

I give the same specs here as with British IPAS, but note that North American craft-brewers stick more closely to specification than do British brewers. As with Pale Ale, North American brewers now thoroughly dominate this style. Once again, North American brewers tend to use Pacific North west hops and grains. Within North America, northwestern brewers hop at much higher rates than do Eastern brewers. It's a regional preference and distinction.

Color 8–14SRM, 16–30EBU; 5.0–7.5% ABV; 1050–10700G; bitterness 40–60IBUS.

Note the decline from a 1979 Ballantines Old India Pale Ale at 10760G and 7.7% ABV.

Strong Ales

It is nearly impossible to properly classify all the beers that fall in to this category, so it has been broken in two, Strong Golden and Strong.

Strong Golden–Belgium

The world-classic beer of this category is Moortgat Brewery's *Duvel*, which means Devil. When the brewer changed (in 1970) its color from deep brown to straw, they created a whole new category. Sometimes it is mistaken for a strong Pilsner. Duvel's triumph has prompted other brewers to make beers in this style, which is singularly Belgian.

Highly aromatic Saaz and Styrian hops gives it its zesty bouquet, a distinctive yeast gives it a delicate fruitiness and, to achieve the light color, only the most lightly-malted barley is used.

It throws such a big foamy head upon opening, that a special extra-wide-mouthed glass is used to contain it.

Give this beer a chance and appreciate it for what it is.

Old Ale–England

Contrary to its name, Old Ales are not beers that have gone stale. Rather, they are beers that are brewed to high alcoholic strengths not normally seen today, especially in North America.

Old Ales, in Britain, are in the medium-strong style. Color range is amber to copper to medium brown. Body should be medium to full, with malt and, often, caramel sweetness. The style possesses much character imparted by esters in the nose and on the palate, which are often described as ripe fruit. Though malty, hop bitterness should be evident, and balanced. Alcohol warming should be noticeable.

Color 10–16SRM; 1050–650G, 5.5–6.5% ABV; bitterness 30–40IBUS; 20–35EBC.

Remember that just because the label says "Old" somewhere on it, that does not necessarily mean that its contents are an Old Ale.

Note: in Australia dark ale is called "old ale".

Strong Ale–England

These beers are dark gold to copper to amber colored with an alcohol range of 1065–1090OG, 6.5–11.0% ABV.

Barleywine–England

This is a sub-style of Strong Ales. It is a matter of choice as to whether a brewery names beers of this profile Barleywine or Strong Ale. Beers in this category are malty and vinous on the palate, obviously strong, indicated by moderate to intense alcohol warming at the back of the mouth. Hop bitterness should be some-what apparent, but far from assertive, as this is a malty style. Pale and dark versions are brewed.

Color range is 20–40SRM; alcohol content 1075–11500G, 7.5–11.0% ABV, or greater; bitterness 45–100 IBUS.

Barleywine–North America craft

Similar to its British cousin, but often using North American-grown ingredients such as hops, 2-row barley and other malts. Brewing sugar, molasses, and even maple syrup may be used. Because of the high alcohol content of this style (British and North American), several yeasts are often used. Initially, a conventional ale yeast, followed by a wine or champagne yeast, once the ale yeast ceases to work.

Specifications are the same as British Barleywine: color range is 20–40SRM; alcohol content 1075–11500G, 7.5–11.0% ABV, or greater; bitterness 45–100 IBUS.

Dubbel and Trippel–Belgium

Dubbels (doubles) are commonly dark, medium-strong, sweet and mellow. They date from the Middle Ages, but their range of original extract is now restricted to 1063–10700g. *Tripels* (triples) are often pale, very strong, full-bodied, well-rounded and bitter.

Dubbels have 6–7.5% ABV, and bitterness of 18–25IBUS. The color range is dark amber to brown. Their aromas are sweet and malty with a very faint hoppy note. They are never hoppy-tasting. Their bodies can be full, but some are a bit thin.

Trippels originated at the Westmalle Abbey. They are the easiest of Belgian styles to classify because they have a very narrow profile. They are blond, just a little darker than a Pilsner, but their aromas range from neutral to estery to malty to sweet; sometimes with a very peppery Goldings hop-aroma, if any hops are present at all. Taste is almost always very neutral, but with generous mouth-feel. The finish is quite sweet with alcoholic warming, but very little alcoholic taste. Some may have a bitter aftertaste imparted by the yeast. Alcohol content is 7–10% ABV. Bitterness is 20–25IBUS.

It is said that Trippels got their name from the fact that they are three times the strength of Specials, which are really the weakest pale ales in the brewery's product line.

Belgian Strong Ales are some of the most enjoyable beers to drink, though they are an acquired taste. It is a huge jump from a Pilsner to any beer in this group.

Extra-strong Ale–England

Extra Strong ales are classified, here, as all Pale Ales with >9% ABV. The profiles of beer in this category are rather broad. Virtually each beer could have its own unique category.

Trappist and Abbey beers are not included in this, or the Extra Strong Dark Ales styles. Abbey beers stand alone.

Scotch Ale–Scotland & Belgium

Scotch ales usually have a malty character and are strong (7.0–10.0% ABV). The style is a first cousin to English Old Ales.

"Scotch Ale", used as a term, implies a very dark, thick, creamy, malty ale with a high alcohol content. It is now produced in Belgium, where it has gained high status, and in France, with an alcohol content of 7–8% ABV. It's introduction in these two countries is thought to have been during the 1914–18 war when it was brewed for British servicemen. There are now more Scotch Ales brewed in Belgium than in Scotland, where it has fallen out of favor.

Color 10–25SRM; bitterness 25–35IBUS; alcohol content 1072–85, 6.2–8.0% ABV, (though they may be brewed stronger, especially in North America).

Bière de Garde–France

These are lovely French beers from the northern provinces of Flanders, Artois, and Picardie, along its Belgium border. Many farmers in that area brewed for themselves and their workers.

The term, *Bière de Garde*, was originally applied to strong, amber- or copper-colored beer. It means 'beer to keep', which implies that the beer is aged a substantial period before being drunk. They are conditioned in corked champagne-style wire-wrapped bottles, after spending several months, or more, maturing in casks. Attenuation is fairly high from the long maturation. This style is filtered, but not pasteurized. They are a blend of pale and dark malts in the mash. However, there are blonde versions, as well, and some are now bottom-fermented.

The body is medium to full, and some alcohol warming may be apparent. Malt, fruitiness, a certain amount of earthiness, and spices, especially pepper, are clearly evident on the palate.

Color 30–35EBC; bitterness 24–29IBUS; alcohol content 1060–760G, 6.5–8.5 ABV.

Note: see the Bière de Noel listing for a seasonal variant of this interesting French style.

Dark Ale

Mild–England

In Britain, Mild is a low-alcohol, dark brown beer, though some are copper-colored. Alcohol content ranges 3.0–3.6% ABV. They are light to medium-bodied, malty, sweet and lightly hopped, and should not be confused with southern-style English Brown ale. Mild is a true "session" beer meant to be drunk in great

amounts. Though they may be bottled, they are at their best as cask-conditioned draft.

Brown Ale–England

This is one of the broadest categories, by style definition, of all the beer styles, though not many brewers produce it. They range in color from amber to deep brown (though not black). Their taste is mild to assertive. English Bullion, Fuggles and Goldings hops are used. Alcohol content is 3.0–4.5% ABV.

There are actually two distinct types of this style. The first could be called Southern English Brown. This type is mild, sweet and very dark. 1031–410G but, more typically, 1030–350G.

The second is the Northern English Brown. This is dryer-tasting, red-brown colored, and a little stronger, with Samuel Smith Nut Brown Ale weighing in at 1049OG. Typical range is 1044–500G. It is more often found in bottle than cask.

As with many ales, their alcohol content has fallen during this century. There are historical references to Brown Ales with OGs at 1055 and 60IBUs bittering.

Brown Ale–North America craft

This North American version is closest to Northern British Brown Ale. However, the North American version tends to be brewed with higher alcohol content, which is fairly typical of most transplanted British styles, and even stronger hop bittering. This style was first developed by home-brewers who made Brown Ales stronger and hoppier than the British specifications. It was previously called Texas (or California) Brown depending on local habit.

Color ranges from deep copper to medium brown. Hop aroma should be readily evident, and hop bitterness should be predominant on the palate, and nearly overwhelm any estery and fruity notes. Body should be medium.

Color 15–22SRM, 35–90EBC; bitterness 20–60IBUS; alcohol content 1040–500G, 4.0–5.9% ABV.

Porter/Entire

This profile will, obviously, be a thoroughly modern one. It is not narrowly defined. Superficially Porter looks like Stout. Indeed, Stout developed from Porter, and was originally called Stout Porter. While Stout should be black, traditional Porter should never be darker than a deep dark brown with hints of red because it should not contain roasted barley and black grains which give Stout its black color and distinct flavor profile.

Porter should, above all, have a full-bodied malty flavor with enough alcohol to give it the desired amount of balance and warmth. Low original gravity beers quickly get out of balance with the hops bitterness and roasted malt flavors standing out too much. Hop aroma should not be overdone. There should be grainy and malty notes and, possibly, some ester-based hints of fruit, and burnt pungent aromas from the roast malt used.

Alcohol content range is 4.5–6.0% ABV, 1045–1060OG, bitterness 25–45IBUS

A last note on Porter. There has actually been a recent cleave in the Porter style. On one hand there are the traditional Porters, as described above, with which some brewers are staying. On the other, there is what I call, Modern Porter. This latter style is characterized as: being very dark to black, like Stout; and, perhaps, a weaker Stout, but without the roasted barley used in Stout, and less hop bittering, say, 38IBUS instead of 60IBUS.

Again, because this is a re-emerging style, some brewers are introducing beers with "ball park" Porter/Stout characteristics and branding them Porters.

Stouts

A S PREVIOUSLY STATED, Porter gave birth to Stout. This was a case where the son surpassed, then overwhelmed the father.

Stout contains highly roasted grains and roasted unmalted grain, which traditional Porter doesn't. Stout is much darker (in some cases black) than Porter. Some modern Porters are made with the same grains as Stout, but in lesser amounts. The two styles tend to somewhat overlap (the naming habits of different brewers tend to fog the issue). One could say that the father (Porter) got to see his son (Stout) grow into a strong healthy man, but never got to see his first-born grandson, a near spitting image of himself (modern Porters).

By the mid-nineteenth century, Stout had become Ireland's national beer. Stout and Ireland are as associative as Lager and Germany or Pale Ale and England. The Stout from Guinness is world famous.

There are four main Stout styles: Dry Stout, Sweet Stout, Double Stout and Imperial Stout. In the British Isles, Dry Stout's 4% ABV, 1040–10460G. In North America it is a little more. A more common brand of Guinness is its bottled Extra Stout, which has a 10550G, 5.4% ABV.

In some tropical countries it reaches 8% ABV. Hopping rate is 55–62IBUS.

Sweet Stout or English Milk Stout usually contains lactose (milk sugar, hence its name). Sweet Stout is much lower in gravity and, therefore, alcohol content than Dry Stout–1044–480G, 3.7–3.8% ABV. Color is a very dark amber.

There is a sub-category of Sweet Stout called Oatmeal Stout that, as its name states, uses some oats or flaked oats in its recipe.

Imperial Stouts, so named because they were brewed for some of the Crown Heads of Europe, have Barleywine proportions (>10740G). Indeed, they have Barleywine taste characteristics that do not resemble Stout's. Here, again, it is a matter of what the brewer decides to name his beers. There is a citation of an Imperial

Stout with a 1094OG, and a Russian Imperial Stout with a 1105OG, and a bitterness of 140IBUS (estimated). Both are enormous by present-day beer standards, even by Stout standards. It is not a beer one would ordinarily find stocked on the local beer merchant's shelves. A commercial example is Samuel Smith Imperial Stout.

I call attention to the very high hop bittering rates used in both Porters and Stouts. High hop bittering rates are essential to make these beers drinkable. With rates similar to Pilsners or Pales Ales, Porters and Stouts would be so out-of-balance to the malt/sweet side of the field as to be sickeningly sweet. Conversely, an American Lager with the bittering rate of a Stout would be even more undrinkable, even to lovers of hoppy tasting beer.

Strong Mild–England

This is a now-rare original English style with parameters similar to Old Ale. They are ruby red to dark brown in color, malty and moderately strong, but are not highly attenuated. Alcohol content of this style should be around 6.0% ABV. This, and its weaker sibling are just now being introduced in the States by more-adventurous brewers

Seasonal ale

IN MANY EUROPEAN countries and Great Britain, brewing seasonal beers is a long-lived tradition. The Belgians are lucky in that their brewers brewed special beers for all the seasons, while in Great Britain their specialty beer season was at Christmas and the winter. It was a tradition that nearly died, but it has been reviving itself during the past twenty years or so, coincidental with their renewed interest in 'real ales' (thanks to the efforts of the Campaign for Real Ale (CAMRA). I have noticed an upswing in advertisements in *What's Brewing* the past few years. Both the Dutch and the Germans brew strong special lagers. The Dutch have taken a page from the Belgians by introducing several seasonal ale styles.

Christmas Ale/Winter Warmers, etc.

This style has exploded in popularity, even in the United States, as more and more breweries, especially the micros, have introduced them. They tend to be dark and have an alcohol content >6.0% ABV. Many use herbs and spices as well.

The Christmas Ales of Flanders are somewhat comparable with British Barley Wines. Others are Scotch Ale derived.

The Dutch, it seems, have no tradition of winter beers. However, brewers, being businessmen, have not let the Belgian success with the Christmas Ales go unnoticed and, therefore, are beginning to introduce their own variations. Traditions have to start somewhere. If you don't have your own, borrow them from someone else and modify them.

Bière de Noel–France

This style is a special darker, richer, and stronger version of Bières de garde brewed especially for the Christmas season, as the name implies.

Saison

These are brewed during the spring, when it is still cool in the North of France and Walloonia in Belgium, for summertime consumption. They are remarkably refreshing, as they should be, since they are meant for warm-weather relief. They are very well attenuated and have a high hop rate to preserve them. Alcohol range is 4.5–8.0% ABV. Color ranges from amber- to copper- to medium brown-colored, with a very big head that leaves good lacing down the side of the glass. Taste varies, with the body ranging from firm to completely thin. The best Saisons have a lovely balanced palate of sweet fruitiness and refreshing sourness, and a clean mellow finish. Saisons are most often naturally conditioned in corked wine bottles (0.75–1.0l).

Some brewers have begun to produce Saisons year-round, causing them to begin to lose their seasonal identity.

Bière de Mars, Traditional, presently obsolete–Belgium

Mars means March in French. March signified the month in the brewing season when Mars brewing stopped. It was produced from the second mashings of the grains during the brewing process. The first (and stronger) wort was used to make Gueuze and the second, weaker runnings were used to make Faro and Mars.

Mars had about 3.0% ABV. I refer to Mars in the past tense because it is no longer made, modern brewing practices making it obsolete. Indeed, it is hard to find any lengthy printed references to it in modern brewing books. I've included it here since I am, after all, trying to be as complete as possible.

Bière de Mars–France

It seems this style is reviving in France thanks to enterprising brewers who have taken a renewed interest in this style.

The classic Brasserie d'Annoeullin, Picardie, founded in 1905, brews a wonderful amber beer to this style at 5.5% ABV using caramel malt.

Other seasonal ale

Though many beers are brewed for a Season such as Christmas/New Year's, Lent/Easter, autumn harvest, etc, beers in this style need not be brewed only for a particular season, but I would like to include, here, special events, also. This might encompass Anniversary Beers, Birthday Beers, Centennial events, The-President-Comes-to-Town Beer, and so on. A brewer might brew a special batch for the birth of his first son: toss it in here. Let this be a catch-all style with Ale and Lager sub-styles.

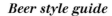

Wheat beer

Wheat has been used in brewing for centuries. It is not as versatile and more limiting than barley, but has useful purposes, the most useful being that it aids in head retention and head size. The Germans and the Belgians have done the most to promote Wheat Beer as a style unto itself, with concentrations running upwards to 75%. American brewers, also, are introducing more wheat beers. The latter tend to be oftentimes refreshing, but lacking interesting aroma and taste characteristics of Belgian and German styles. This is a case of it all being in the yeasts used.

The four major categories are North German Wheats, Bayerisch Wheats, Belgian Wits, and New American Wheats.

Besides the fact that they share several styles within their group, wheat beer can also be sub-divided by whether or not they are filtered, or have yeast still in bottle (*mit hefe*, in German).

Berliner Weisse (white)–Germany

Called the *Champagne du Nord* by French soldiers during the Napoleonic wars, Berliner Weisse is an extremely dry, sharp, tart and refreshing beer. It is an ideal hot-summer-days beer. The tartness comes from a healthy dose of lactobacillus combined with its yeast and a high (67–75%) wheat content, not from hops. In fact, the hopping rate of these beers is very low–4–15IBUs. Too, they have a very low alcohol content–2.5–3.7% ABV, which has been scaled down from the 4.4% they were at the end of the last century. The color is very pale, and they are clear, if you are careful not to pour out the yeast sediment with the beer.

To be a legal "Berliner" Weisse, in Germany, the beer must be brewed within the city of Berlin. It has been noted as a style as far back as 1572, but it rose to popularity at the end of the 1800s when

Berlin was an Imperial city. The style has also been called "Champagne of the Spree" (the Spree, a river that flows through Berlin, the German capitol).

They are most often and best served in wide-mouthed glasses because they are very frothy. A shot or dash of sweetened fruit (raspberry being the favorite) or woodruff syrup is traditionally added. Or the inside of the glass may be first coated with syrup and then the beer poured into it.

Color 2–4SRM, 5–10EBC; bitterness 4–15IBUS;1028–32OG, 2.5–3.7% ABV.

Weisse–North Germany

This is a category for Weissebier not brewed in Berlin. Not much of a difference here, except that the alcohol content may be as high as 5.0% ABV. Wheat content is 35–75%. These are not necessarily as sour and tart as are their Berliner cousins.

Grätzerbier–Germany

This style, as does Berliner Weisse, has a low alcohol content, but is much more highly hopped than its Berlin cousin. Grätzerbier is made up of two-thirds highly-roasted wheat malt and one-third pale barley malt. These first three styles of north German wheat beers illustrates a regional difference in tastes when compared to south German wheat beers.

Bitterness 50IBUS; alcohol content 1030–34OG, 3.0–3.4% ABV.

Weizen-Weissbier, Kristal Klar–Germany

This is a South German/Bavarian style that differs considerably from North German and Belgian styles. South Germany encompasses Bayern and Baden-Württemberg. The heads are big and creamy in both styles. Carbonation is very high. Therefore, a slow steady pour is necessary.

Weizenbier usually use different, distinctive yeast strains that impart a blend of apples and citrus fruit notes in the aroma and a clove-like or nutmeg-like taste. Smokey and vanilla notes may also be present. Wheat content is 40–70%, and barley malt, similar to North German Weissebier, but they also include, in some brands, dark and roasted wheat and barley malts. Some writers and guides state wheat content should be "at least 50%", but German texts I have indicate the correct range is as stated above. The hop rate is low, intruding only slightly into the profile. Though normally well-attenuated, body should be medium. The majority are very pale- to pale-colored, filtered and crystal clear. This last item does not apply to Dunkelweizen and Weizenbock beers.

Color 3–9SRM, 8–16EBC; bitterness 10–19IBUS; alcohol content 1046–56OG, 4.5–5.7% ABV.

Weizen-Weissbier, mit hefe–Germany

The same as above, except unfiltered. If the yeast is poured out with the beer, this version will be cloudy and have a yeast flavor and a fuller mouthfeel. As it is a distinct style, it should have its own category.

Weizen taken with the yeast has developed into an extremely popular style among health-conscious Germans and others in the know. A side benefit of live yeast is that it has a marvelous flushing effect on the digestive tract.

Dunkel Weizenbier-Dunkel Weissbier–Germany

These are darker colored variations of normal Weizenbier. The phenolic and estery characteristics of weissbier remain, and added to that are sweet maltiness, roasted malt, and chocolate notes on both the palate and the nose. Color ranges from copper-brown to dark brown. All the other parameters are very close or unchanged.

Color 16–23SRM, 35–96EBC; bitterness 10–15IBUS; alcohol content 1048–56OG, 4.8–5.4% ABV.

Steinweizen–Germany

Here is a rare and unusual style: a German wheat beer brewed by use of super-heated stones. See Steinbier for further description of the process used by the Rauchenfels Brauerei.

The one example I have has a low 3.5% ABV. It is a very lively beer, and a bit sharper than Rauchenfels Steinbeer. Aromas and palate characteristics are burnt and smoky grain. Wheat makes up 60% of the grist. The finish is big, as would be expected and spicy, with phenolic notes.

Weizenbock–Germany

Bockbier, a lager, is, in Germany, defined as having at least 1066OG, 6.6% ABV. The range is 6.25 to 6.9% ABV. Weizenbockbier is brewed to the Bockbier requirements, but remains an ale. Color is pale to dark They normally are considerably darker than light-colored weizenbier. The amount of wheat used ranges from 40–60%. Malty on the palate, with banana, chocolate, vanilla, and clove notes in both aroma and palate. This is a complex and well-rounded style.

Weizen Doppelbock–Germany

As Doppelbock is to Bockbier, so Weizen Doppelbock is to Weizenbock. The alcohol range is 7.2–7.5% ABV. Weizen-Doppelbock may be light- or dark-colored (though most are light), with a pronounced barley-malt and wheat-malt aroma and mild hops bittering. Both styles may come clear or they may have yeast in the bottle.

Witbier, Bière Blanche (White beer)–Belgium & Holland

This style was well-defined over 100 years ago but, like Porter, it has all but disappeared. The last of 30 original brewers closed in 1954. It was reintroduced in 1966 by Pierre Celis, who bought the De Kluis Brouwerij in Hoegaarden. Then, in 1978, with two Dutch partners, he bought an old factory that used to produce lemonade and converted it into a brewery. There was an unfortunate brewery fire in 1985, requiring substantial cost to rebuild. Their insurance wasn't sufficient. Interbrew, the largest Belgian brewery, backed him in his rebuilding efforts. Eventually Mr. Celis sold the brewery to Interbrew, but they retained his services with a contract that eventually expired in 1990. Interbrew now controls a majority of that country's beer market. There are 14 other Belgian brewers now producing Witbier–quite a turnabout in 37 years.

For those curious about the fate of Mr. Celis, not to worry. He moved to the United States, and opened the Celis Brewery on a seven-acre site in Austin, Texas. He now produces a Grand Cru, White, Pale Bock and a Golden, all bearing his name. Life has a strange way of casting ironies about. Mr. Celis is now back in Belgium, with Christine, his daughter, who is president of the firm, selling his White Beer, under contract to his native countrymen. It was she who encouraged him to do this. The 40% duty levied by Belgium on American beer prohibits him exporting his Witbier to Belgium.

Witbier was originally meant to be bottled or casked within four or five days after completion of primary fermentation, and consumed within two weeks. If not, it went quickly acidic and sour. During cool weather months, it could last, perhaps, four or five weeks.

Witbier is pronounced wheat beer, but means White Beer. In French the name is *Bière blanche*. The name derives from its clearly evident milky haze. This is because the particles in suspension are too light-weight to settle out, as happens in most other beers. The haze is from reflected light off the particles.

Witbier's main characteristics are that they are white (no, not like milk) cloudy, and highly carbonated, which produces a dense enormous head. When on, they are a refreshing drink.

As with most Belgian brews, hops play a minor role. Brewers use hops aged one to three years, aiming for their preservative properties, not their bittering or aromatic ones.

Witbier or Biére Blanche–North America craft

Similar to the Belgian style, but the use of American Cascade and Willamette hops (the later a Fuggle variety) begs for a new style to be named.

In time more North American microbreweries and regional breweries will begin brewing beers to this style, when they see the increasing popularity of Wits, and the continuously improving tastes of North American beer drinkers.

Wheat beer–North America

Strangely, other beer writers I am aware of have not given this style its own classification, considering its lack of similarities to European wheat styles. North American Wheat is a freshly developing style that is different than the taste profiles of German Weizenbier. The distinction is due, in the main to different wheat strains grown in North America than in Europe, and to different yeast strains utilized. Additionally, North American brewers feel no compulsion to match European wheat beer styles. Instead, they are experimenting and developing their own. At present, the style is in its infancy so there are no set parameters, but I can give you some sample characteristics. Original gravities seem to be staying in the 1040–50 range; alcohol content 4.0–5.0% ABV; bitterness 15–20IBUs; colors range from gold to dark.

Many brewpubs and some microbreweries, using equipment best suited to brewing ales, are cleverly using light-colored examples of this style as a substitute for light-colored lagers, color being similar for both. Dark examples may substitute for North American Dark Larger.

Wild Yeast Beers

THESE BEERS ARE the only ones of their kind in the world. They are composed of 40% unmalted wheat and 60% malted barley (this is a general parameter). They are fermented by spontaneous fermentation to airborne yeasts and bacteria. The base Lambic is a component part of many Fruit Beers and has several versions. They could be included in the Wheat Beer category, but because of their unique fermentation method, they deserve and are acknowledged a category all their own. A pure Lambic has very low carbonation; Vieux (Old) Lambic from Brasserie Cantillon, cited as a perfect example of the style, has no carbonation. Almost all the brewed Lambic is used to make Gueuze and Fruit Lambics, but some is sold as Lambic Doux (Sweet), Lambic Vieux or Faro. If a Lambic less than six months old, it is often labelled as Jong (Young) or Vos (Fox) Lambic.

Lambic wort is usually boiled a minimum of three hours. Sometimes it is boiled and then simmered overnight, quite in contrast with normal one to two hour boils given other beer worts. Aged hops two to three years old are exclusively used. The idea is to avoid hop aromas, but to extract their preservative or antiseptic components.

Lambics are brewed in and around (out to about 20km) Brussels. The area where the proper air-borne yeasts and bacteria exist is limited to this region. There is no complicated explanation. It is simply a quirk of nature. That is not to say that somewhere else in the world similar conditions do not exist. It's simply that no other brewers have experimented: failure is expensive, and the taste of these beers are so very different from ales and lagers that enticing drinkers to accept Lambic beers would be long-term and difficult.

Note that many Lambics are aged two years or so. Vieux Lambic is aged for three years in cask and another in bottle. It is pink-tinted Sherry-colored and has nearly no carbon dioxide.

Faro (also called Faro-Lambic)–Belgium

These are young Lambics made from blending moderate-strength worts, or high-strength and low-strength worts and sweetened with candi sugar. They are sometimes colored with caramel, and diluted with water. Usually they are less than one year old.

Alcohol content 4.5–5.5% ABV.

Gueuze–Belgium

Gueuze is a blend of Lambic beer of different ages which are bottle fermented. The best Gueuzes are an equal blend of one-, two- and three-year-old Lambics. They are coarsely filtered after blending and then bottled. In addition, the newly bottled Gueuze should be laid down for nine months spanning one summer (meaning a cool and a warm period). The temperature changes are necessary because the several yeasts and bacteria do their best work at different temperatures. Too high a temperature can damage traditional bottle-conditioned Gueuze because they are still alive. They have to be carefully handled and stored. Owing to hot weather in 1931, over 3m bottles of Gueuze were destroyed in Brussels.

Some brewers make their Gueuze in bulk, subject it to cold-filtration, flash-pasteurization and artificial carbonation before bottling.

Brewers of this style often use Gueuze, rather than Faro, as a base for other styles, especially Fruit Beers.

The name derives from the Guezenstraet or rue des Gueux in Brussels. In French, Gueux means beggar.

Color 6–13SRM; 15–33EBC; bitterness 11–23IBUS; alcohol content 1044–56OG, 5.0–5.5% ABV;.

Lambic Doux–Belgium

In English, 'soft lambic'. This is a clear, filtered, nearly flat Lambic with brown sugar added as a sweetener, which takes some getting used to. It sold at cafés in Brussels.

Lambic Blanche Wit–Belgium

This hybrid style was introduced in 1993 by Timmermans, an enterprising Belgian brewer. This definition of hybrid, as used here connotes a blend of two different style beers. It is not the same definition as Ale-Lager and Lager Ale hybrids. This style is made by blending old Lambic with young Witbier. Additionally, it may be made with or without fruit.

Style parameters have not been set. The one example recorded so far has an alcohol content of 4.0% ABV.

Expect other brewers to follow suit and introduce their own interpretations of this new style.

Other Ales

Tafelbier-Bière de Table–Belgium & France

This is a style that is in danger of being replaced by NABLABs (No Alcohol Beers-Low Alcohol Beers), which are heavily promoted and profitable for their brewers. *Tafelbier* is Flemish for Table Beer. In French it is called *Bière de Table*. Tafelbier is a sweet, low-alcohol beer. They are made with the second or third run-offs from the mash tank. The result is a low-gravity wort, which in turn produces a low-alcohol beer: ≤3.0% ABV. In Belgium, they are classified as Category III beers with 1004–1016OG, and account for about 3.5% of beer production.

This style is similar to the English Mild, but tends to be even less alcoholic. Sadly, they are both in periods of decline.

Grand Cru and Cuvée–Belgium

This is a slightly difficult style to pin down because it has been suggested that the names attached to the brands are not always accurate. *Grand Cru,* meaning Special Vintage, are meant to be the brewer's favorite or best beer. These were most often used for special occasions, such as weddings, victory celebrations, grand openings with the town mayor in attendance, etc. They were used much the way champagne is in other countries: as a special something not meant to be had everyday. Grand Crus were brewed in smaller quantities, or shorter brew lengths than regular brands.

Tim Webb, writing in the *Good Beer Guide to Belgium and Holland* says this about Grand Cru/Cuvée:

"The terms *'Cuvée'* and *'grand cru'* are frequently applied to a wide variety of beers in Belgium and the Netherlands. However, the terms are worse than useless to the consumer. They say nothing about the beer in the bottle except to imply that it will be expensive.

"Cuvée" is commonly used in the names of label beers, regular brewery ales, which are masquerading under a false name for a particular distributor. One Dutch bar owner told the Guide that "grand cru" means "big crutch" and is used either to suggest machismo or else because the beer is so puny that it needs extra support!

"The Guide uses neither term in classifying a beer's style."

A fairly strong indictment.

One can also look at these as either pumped up Old Ales or as Strong Ales.

It would be very easy to simply toss these into the Strong Ale group, but there is a problem: labeling. I prefer to retain this category, but point out that these beers are, indeed, Strong Ales. Too, since many of these are aged for prolonged periods, it wouldn't do them justice to simply toss them into the general Strong Ale group, where, perhaps, they might get lost or marginalized.

Dampfbier–Germany

This is another specialty beer, like *Steinbier*, from German. It is likewise, undergoing a revival of sorts, though I don't assume it will ever become hugely popular.

The style is very fruity, and the brand from Maisel Bräu has vanilla undertones. It is made using four malts, and hopped with Hallertauer. Alcohol content is about 5.0% ABV. *Dampfbier* is paler and with more a reddish cast than, say, an Altbier from Düßeldorf.

As Anchor Brewing has done with its Steam Beer, Maisel's Dampfbier name is registered and not meant to indicate a style, though it is in its own right. Comparing Anchor Steam Beer to Dampfbier, the latter is made using different production techniques and, too, has an entirely different profile.

Steinbier–Germany

This style is very old in the making. One can just imagine some of the earliest German brewers super-heating stones (nowadays at 1,200°C) and placing them in the wort to bring it to the boil. The reason for using heated stones in this manner was because the style dates to before the advent of iron vessels. The ones made of wood could not be directly heated with fire, and this was the solution of these early brewers.

To continue, but in the present tense, the stones are then removed from the wort. Both are cooled and fermentation begins. The stones are then replaced in the wort and the yeast attacks the crystallized sugars that concentrated on the stones within seconds. A violent secondary fermentation quickly begins. It gradually subsides during the ensuing three weeks. What results is a light mouth watering beer with definite smoked tones. It is smooth and somewhat dry.

The style nearly went extinct, but this very rare beer is undergoing a bit of a revival. In 1982, Gerd Borges, then brewing in Neustadt near the ex-East German frontier, decided to revive it as a way to increase sales. Production has since moved to the Schwabian town of Marktoberdorf near Coburg, where it brews a Steinbier simply named Rauchenfels Steinbier.

In Germany, this and *Rauchbier* are described variously as "new specialty beers" or "new Old Beers". Too, more marketing effort and money are being put into them.

Fruit beer

Fruit has been added to beer in Belgium for over 400 years. Cherries and raspberries are the primary fruit used, though not the only ones.

There are several styles of fruit beer. Some have been going through change during the past few years, as many Belgian brewers have taken to making these beers sweeter than they naturally and traditionally have been, much to the chagrin of afficionados.

Fruit can be added in several ways. The best is to use the whole fruit, which may be added to the wort, or later, to fermented beer, where it provokes additional fermentation because of their sugar content. Second, a combination of whole fruit and fruit juice may be used. The juice is used to attain final balance in the beer.Third, no whole fruit is used, just fruit juice. The more juice is used, the more fruity the bouquet. Additionally, the use of fruit greatly alters the color of the base beer.

Belgians make no style distinction between fruit beers made with different base styles. This is confusing, so here they are listed separately. There are three styles that make the base of fruited beers. They are Lambic, Gueuze, and Old Ale.

The color range of these beers is dark copper to medium brown with tints of red because of the fruit used. Alcohol content is about 4.0–6.2% ABV for the gueuze-based brands; 5.0% ABV for the Lambic-based ones; and 5.5–6.7% ABV for those based on Ould Brune.

Kriek (Cherry) Lambic–Belgium

This ale is called *Kriek* in Belgium, their word for the fruit. There are several varieties of cherries that are used, though the Schaerbeek variety is preferred because it is not sweet.

The profile will be as the base beer, though perhaps with a slight increase in alcohol content, as the fruit sugars would increase it. Color ranges from red to deep ruby red, and fruit is clearly evident in the nose.

Frambozen (Raspberry) Lambic–Belgian

Raspberry (*Framboise* in French, *Frambozen* in Flemmish) is the fruit of choice for this style. It is also called *Framboos* in some locales. There are lovely fruit notes in the nose, and a long, refreshing finish.

There is notable Framboise brewed by Brasserie Cantillon called Rosé de Gambinus. Brasserie Cantillon is the only gueuze brewery in the Brussels area.

Peche (Peach) Lambic–Belgium

Peche is the French word for peach, and is used on labels. That is the fruit used is this style. One might question its use, but it makes a very refreshing beer even more so.

Kriek (Cherry) Gueuze–Belgium

As the name implies, this style is a Gueuze with cherry fruit or juice (also called essence). The best examples are those that use the most whole fruit.

Frambozen (Raspberry) Gueuze–Belgium

Similar to Kriek Gueuze, but with raspberry as the fruit of choice. All these fruit beers are absolutely delicious. For those who enjoy wine, fruit beers are an easy gateway to beer with distinct taste.

Ould Kriek (Old Cherry)–Belgium

Called *Ould Kriekenbier* in Belgium, this is a blend of Ould Brune Ale (Old Brown) and cherries. The cherries, to a remarkable degree, enhance the sour notes already present in Ould Brune. Some of these brands are world-class, and all are worth trying.

Thankfully, these are not as rare in the States as they used to be.

Ould Frambozen (Old Raspberry)–Belgium

Called *Ould Frambozen*, this raspberry-fruited beer is a sister of Ould Kriek. It is more a matter of preference as to which fruit beer one would like over the others. Why not be open-minded and enjoy all of them?

Other Fruit Beers

This was once the realm of home brewers. None but them dared brew such beer, for there seemed to be very little commercial demand (though demand can always be created). The Belgian brewer, Keersmaeker, does produce a lovely fruit beer called Mort Subite Cassis. Black currents are used. The aroma is massive, the palate is of bitter-sweet fruit, and the finish is lingering

Home-brewers, who are better able to experiment than are commercial brewers, experiment with every type (especially berry) fruit. Some are better than others, with citrus fruit and apple lending themselves poorly to beer making. That said, several Lemon Lagers and Apple Ales have recently appeared. Blueberries, blackberries, strawberries, currents, and others have been used.

In the States, it appears beers of this style sprang from brew-pubs and some micro-breweries whose head-brewers had home-brewing roots. Ever experimental, they've taken chances based on the knowledge that fruited home-brews they made were favorably received by those with whom they've shared, or had judge them. The base styles to which fruit is added include North American Lager, Pale Ale, Belgian Brown, Stout, and Wheat beers.

Expect to see many more fruited beers come to market. However, I must give *caveat emptor.* The tastes are not always up to Belgian standards, and some may disappoint. There are several reasons for this. Firstly, fruited beers should be aged to allow for maturing, mellowing, and blending of all the elements. Beer dosed with fruit extract at bottling doesn't allow for this all-important stage. Secondly, fresh fruit added to the fermenter is better than fruit extract, though more difficult to work with. Finally, hop tastes clash, sometimes disastrously, with fruit. Belgian brewers know this. That is why they use two-to-three year old hops that have lost their bittering components.

Spiced Beers

In several countries, the United States and Belgium included, spiced beers are being re-introduced.

Essences, herbs, spices and other flavorings have long been used to flavor and/or preserve beer, especially in the times before the wide-spread use of hops for the same purposes. For simplicity's sake, I will use the term Spiced Beers to encompass all that fall into this category.

Some narrow-minded beer experts don't even consider Spiced Beers to be true beers but, at best, think of them as ersatz beer. This is too harsh a judgment, especially when one considers these are styles that date back centuries. One can, perhaps, sympathize with German brewers, who are limited by their *Reinheitsgebot,* to using only barley malt, hops yeast and water in their brews.

The beer styles best suited for spicing are higher-gravity Brown Ales, Pale Ales, and sweet-tasting ales, all of which tend to be fairly complex in the first place.

The list of spices going into beers in this group are almost innumerable. A short list:

all-spice, chocolate/cocoa, cinnamon, cloves, coffee, coriander, cumin, curaco, ginger, jalapeño pepper, licorice, molasses, nutmeg, peppermint, spruce and tea.

Ale-Lager hybrids

B EERS, IN THIS sub-category of ales, are brewed using ale yeast, but undergo cold lagering, which differentiates them from pure ales. There are Lager-Ale hybrids, too, which are the opposites of this group. They are listed in the Lager section.

Pils Ale–the Netherlands

This is a unique style some Dutch breweries are developing. It is like a Pilsner-style lager, but it is brewed with ale yeast. These are comparable to Kölsch, but are not like a typical Pilsner. Most are a bit darker than one would expect to see in a light-colored Pilsner. Contrarily, they are not like Pale Ales. So, what to do? Come up with a new category. Voila! This style is a cousin to American Steam Beers and to cream ales.

Altbier–Germany

Düßeldorf is the traditional home of Altbier (but not the only place Altbier is brewed in Deutschland). The word "Altbier" is the German term for a top-fermented beer, though alt means old in English. Old, meaning in the old (top-fermenting) manner of brewing. At some breweries, this traditional manner is combined with the modern lager technique of cold aging at 39–41°F. Alts brewed in this latter way may be classified as ale-lager hybrids.

Only by hasty examination can they be compared with British ales. They are as similar as dissimilar. An Englishman would argue that their ales have more individuality, and a German might retort that their Altbiers are cleaner, crisper, and smoother. Altbiers have little of the acidity and fruitiness of British ales. Rather, they have a much cleaner palate, and a complex, well-balanced and intricate blend of hop bitterness and malty body. Altbier is traditionally dispensed from the cask (wooden) as Real Ale.

Two or three German malts (Munich and Vienna) may be used in Altbier brewing. Wheat often is 10–15% of its content, as well as up to 10% crystal malt. Perhaps 1% dark malts are also used. Wort boils are 1.5–2hr.

Classic examples of this style are dark-copper to rich-brown colored, use only pure single-cell yeast strains, are cold conditioned for three to eight weeks. Body is medium, and malt is predominant on the palate. Fruity esters should be low.

Color 11–19SRM, 25–65EBC; bittering 25–50IBUs, alcohol content 1040–500G, 4.0–5.0% ABV.

Kölsch–Germany

This is the hometown drink of metropolitan of Köln (Cologne), Germany, hence its name. Bonn, the German capital, is within this area, located in the industrial north-east. Like Altbier, Kölsch is an ale-lager hybrid–top- and warm-fermented, but cold lagered. Together they make up a minuscule portion of the entire beer production of Germany. If this style is brewed elsewhere but Köln in Germany, under German law, the word Kölsch must be preceded by the name of the city of origin. This is a strictly adhered to German naming practice.

Kölsch is a very pale, golden, highly-hopped beer. It is slightly lactic tasting, too.

In Germany, Kölsch must, by law, be filtered, unless it is labelled as Unfiltered. Lagering is for 14–40 days.

Kölsch is now being brewed in small batches by some adventurous North American craft brewers.

Color 3.5–5SRM, 8–14EBC; bittering 16–34IBUs; alcohol content 1042–470G, 4.4–5.0% ABV.

Native beers

SINCE MAN FIRST brewed beer, wild, airborne yeasts and bacteria have been the agent of fermentation. Not until man gained the prerequisite scientific knowledge and skills was he able to isolate and culture "good" brewing yeasts from the "bad".

Native brewing cultures, wherever they remain today have employed from time the gift of wild yeast. As these are brewed only for immediate family, clan, or tribal consumption, using whatever fermentable grains are at hand, and local plants for flavoring agents, there are no commercial examples to list, or style parameters. However, in the name of completeness, they do deserve mention here.

Native brewing techniques today vary little from when man first brewed several thousand years ago. Remarkably, no matter where the tribes are, whether it be Central and South America, Africa, or Asia, their brewing methods are nearly identical, though results vary.

Modern Western man took native practices and applied science and technology to them. The result is the brewing industry we know today. Belgian Lambic brewers are the close end of the brewing chain stretching back several thousand years. Tribal brewers are at the far end, closest to brewing's birth.

Lagers
Bottom-fermented beer

Lager Beer Styles

Light & Amber Lagers:	Dark Lagers:	Lager-Ale Hybrids:
Standard Lager	Dark Lager	Bok Ales
Light Lager	Old Brown	Malt Liquors
Tropical Light Lager	Dunkles	California Common Beer
Non-Alcohol, Low Alcohol	Schwarzbier (black beer)	Kentucky Common Beer
Economy Beer		Stout Lager
Premium Lager	**Bock Beers:**	Porter Lager
Dry Lager	Doppelbocks	Winter Lagers/Festbier
Ice Lager	Eisbock	Lager Wheat
Continental Lagers	Maibock	
Pilsner, Pilsener, Pils	Meibok	
Diät Pils	Bokbier	
Dortmunder Export	Dubbelbok	
Munich Bayerisches Helles	Bock	
Bière de Paris	Double Bock	
Bière de Garde Lager	Strong Pils	
Märzenbier	Rauchbier	
Wiener (Vienna)		
Amber Lager		

IN EVERY COUNTRY except Great Britain, lager is king. It is Number One, El Supremo, der König, the King. In a very short time, it displaced Ale as the most-brewed beer in the world.

Lager is different from ale in several ways. First, different yeasts, bottom- instead of top-fermenting strains, are used. Second, it is fermented at a lower temperature than ale. Third, it is aged (or lagered, hence its name) much longer, at a much colder temperature than is ale. I am comparing here average lagers and ales such as a Pilsner and a Bitter. There are exceptions to every rule: Belgian

Trappist Ales are aged for up to three years. Fourth, because lager beer is (it should be) kept cold right until it is served to the drinker, it has a longer "shelf-life" than does ale. Cold temperatures help retard spoilage. Fifth, comparing the most commonly drunk lagers to the most popular ales, there is a color difference. The average Pilsner is gold-colored while Bitter or Mild is pale- to copper- to medium-brown-colored. One advantage (or disadvantage) is the misperception among people about beer color. It is commonly held that the darker the beer the stronger it is. This is not true. For example the Belgian Trippel is straw-colored and has an average alcohol content of 9.5% ABV, The copper-colored English Bitter has an average alcohol content of, say, 4.2% ABV. Taken further, the average English Bitter has the same alcohol content range as American Light Lagers (4.2% ABV). For those wondering about calories, their main source is alcohol, so there is really no reason to drink light beers to save weight when for about the same calorie count one could drink a delicious ale.

There are two main groups of lagers. The first is the traditional Czech and German lagers, of which the latter are subject to the *Reinheitsgebot,* the German Beer Purity Laws. These require German beer to be made from only malted barley, hops yeast and water (malted wheat is permitted). Unmalted raw, and roasted grains are not permitted, as are all fruit, herbs, spices and adjuncts. Thus, German beer is the "purest". The second group is lagers brewed elsewhere. Most countries have lax or no brewing laws of which to speak. Practically anything goes: the use of corn, rice, brewing sugars, and other cost-cutting adjuncts; preservatives other than hops; chemical treatments to get essentially dead beer to appear as if it were a German lager, etc. It has been reported that in the ex-East Germany, before unification, brewers were forced by authorities to use cow bile, as a cheap bittering substitute for hops!

I have taken the liberty of cleaving some styles in two. Styles noted as "Style X–North America" contain the mass-produced brands.

To the new styles I have added "Craft" after North America. These include all lagers that are brewed using only hops, malt, water, and yeast. Fruit essence is permitted in those styles.

Light & Amber lager

Standard Lager–North American

North American Lagers are very light colored. Body is light. They are clean, crisp. Carbonation may be described as aggressive. Hop and malt aromas are absent. Hop bitterness is slight, and hop flavor should be negligible to mild.

Corn, rice, and other grains and sugar adjuncts may be used.

Color 2–4SRM, 5–10EBC; bitterness 5–17IBUS; alcohol content 1040–460G, 3.8–4.5 ABV.

Standard Lager–North American Craft Brewed

This is a growing category, one that micro-brewers and pub-brewers have keenly taken to. The first lager from these brewers will, most often, be this style. This is out of necessity. To get their lager into pubs and restaurants they must offer a beer that is similar to that of Standard Lager. When drinkers compare a Craft-brewed lager to a Standard, the craft-brewed wins outright. This accounts for much of the growth micro-brewers and contract brewers have been experiencing.

Alcohol content is >4.5% and frequently is higher, up to the lower limits of a German Bock. There does not seem to be any skimping on the malt here. Color ranges from light to golden amber, and bitterness is comparable with quality Euro-Lagers, ie, 25–40IBUS.

Color 3–5SRM, 8–13EBC; bitterness 18–45IBUS; alcohol content 1045–60, 4.5–6.0% ABV.

Light Lager–North American (low calorie beer)

The U.S. Food and Drug Administration dictates that any beer branded as "Light" (referring to caloric content) must have at least 25% fewer calories than the Standard version of that beer. Sales of this style are hotly contested amongst North American brewers.

Light Lagers are extremely light-colored, highly carbonation, and light-bodied. Flavor may be described as mild, and bitterness is extremely low to low. The finish is very brief.

Color 2–4SRM, 5–10EBC; bitterness 7–19IBUS; alcohol content 1023–1040OG, 2.3–4.4% ABV.

Tropical Light Lager–Oceana, tropical islands

Though their color is in the same range as North American Lager, this style has more bitterness, and a wider range of alcohol content. Adjuncts, such as sugar, corn, rice or other grains are used. Hop aromas are negligible; fruit esters should be low; body is thin; hop bitterness is low to moderate. Because cane sugar is used by some breweries, there may be apple notes in the aroma and on the palate.

Color 2–4SRM, 6–10EBC; bitterness 9–25IBUS; alcohol content 1032–50OG, 2.5–5.6% ABV.

NABLABs–North America

Non-alcohol/low alcohol beers (NABLAB) differ from their Light brothers. The former strives to remove as much unfermentable sugars as possible to reduce calories, but not necessarily alcohol. The latter remove most of the alcohol. By the way, there is no such thing as a completely alcohol-free beer. These usually have <0.5% ABV.

Some NABLABS may be considered tasty because they retain some residual sweetness and hop charter.

Low alcohol beers have <1.6% ABV.

NABLABs–Germany

Germans refer to, and categorize, these beers as *Einfachbier*, which translates as *simple beer*. The root, *einfach*, can also be translated as elementary, easy, plain, ordinary homely and frugal. Einfachbier is designated *Alkoholfrei* (alcohol-free) on labels.

Alcohol content ranges 0.5–1.5% ABV, and their color can be light or dark. They are watery or thin, mild, and are without pronounced character. This, to a German's palate. Compared with North American NABLABS, some of these might even be described as tasty.

To sum up the German attitude towards these beers, I'll quote Dietrich Höllhuber and Wolfgang Kaul, authors of *Die Biere Deutschlands* (The Beers of Germany): "Ask us not how man came to this beer and how he tasted it!" *("Fragen Sie uns nicht, wie man zu diesem Bier kommt und wie es schmeckt!")*

Economy Beer–North America

This style is for inexpensive brands, which are most-often sold in supermarkets, etc.

Alcohol content is 3.2% ABV or less, giving them some advantage in states that encourage low-strength beer in the market. Other characteristics are similar to the Light Lager–North American style.

There is great need in North America for a tastier and more characterful economy beer, in line with English Mild and Belgian Bière de table. In Germany, lagers of this alcoholic strength are not brewed.

Premium Lager–North America

This is a catch-all category. Included are what mega-brewers call their Premium and Super Premium beers.

The big distinction between this style and Standard Lager is that Premium Lagers use fewer adjuncts, 30% versus up to 65%; rice adjunct instead of corn; a little bit of two-row barley malt instead of six-row. Rarely will the brewer use more hops (16 versus 14IBUS). The types of hops used are the same: Cluster, Cascade, Willamette and, on occasion, Hallertauer (domestic or imported), and Saaz for aroma, which is negligible to low. Alcohol content is slightly boosted.

Color 2–8SRM, 5–15EBC; bitterness 13–23IBUS; alcohol content 1046–500G, 4.3–5.0% ABV.

Dry Lager–Japan & North America

This is a new style introduced by Asahi Brewing Company in 1987. Asahi was quickly followed by Kirin, Sapporo and Suntory. The Japanese quickly brought the product to North America, where it was almost immediately duplicated.

The term Dry is really a misnomer. Dry, in this sense, means 'not sweet', not 'not wet'. The term was actually ported over from wine descriptions.

Leave it to the Japanese to genetically engineer a strain of yeast with a special enzyme that converts normally unfermentable dextrins into fermentable sugars. It thus reduces the sweetness.

Alcohol content of these straw-colored Drys is similar to Regular and Premium Lagers. Because the style is so highly-attenuated, alcohol content is a bit higher than the OGs would suggest. Color is about the same as other beer styles in this category. Bitterness is noticeable, and a little more apparent because the style is so lacking in malt sweetness to counter-balance it. Carbonation is aggressive.

Color 2–4srm, 5–10ebc; bitterness 15–23ibus; alcohol content 1040–500g, 4.4–5.5% abv.

Ice Lager–North America

This is the latest style to develop in North America. It seems to be still wriggling about somewhat, as brewers modify and define it. The beer is chilled before filtration until ice crystals form. They may, or may not, be separated, but the result is somewhat higher in alcohol content than Standard North American Lager. The style is completely different, in every way, from German Eisbock.

It is brewed with no, or few, adjuncts. Hop aroma and flavor is low. Body is medium, with some residual malt sweetness.

Color 2–8srm, 5–16ebc; bitterness 7–20ibus; alcohol content 1040–600g, 4.6–6% abv.

Continental Lagers–Europe

Of all the brewers in Europe, only the Germans are constrained by their beer purity laws. The disadvantage is that they cannot make cheaper beer by using less expensive ingredients. On the other hand, what better way to promote the fact that one's beers are pure and unadulterated? There are brewers in Europe, other than the Germans, who adhere to the *Reinheitsgebot*. It is a strong selling point. Besides, their customers like the fact that "their" brewer is producing wholesome, all-natural beer.

These beers arose from the development, in the mid-1800s, of bottom-fermenting, cold-temperature-working yeast strains. These yeasts developed from the long-time brewing practice, in certain regions of Europe such as the mountainous regions of Bavaria, of storing beer in cold caves or caverns. Over time, the yeast adapted to the cold environment by their reuse from batch to batch (this after the discovery of yeast's function in fermentation).

Within about 60 years, lager completely displaced ale, except in Great Britain (as previously mentioned). Europe, where it got its start at different sites, developed their own singular styles. From there, lager-brewing was brought to North America by German immigrants.

Pilsner, Pilsner, Pils–Germany

This is one of the four main lager styles. As its name suggests, Pilsner originated in Pilsen, in the Czech Republic. Pilsner is also interchangeably called Pilsner and Pils.

In Germany, the general parameters of Pilsners are as follows. Alcohol content (typical) 4.8% ABV (range in class 4.8–5.7% ABV); 1044–560G; light to very light color; foamy (white) head; fine hops bitterness; very fine hop aroma. Hop types used are Hallertauer, Northern Brewer, Spalt, or Tettnanger. Water hardness ranges from 200–400ppm.

Pils falls within the German *vollbiere* (full beers) group. There are four German styles: *klassische Pilsner* (Classic Pilsner); *süddeutschen Pilsner* (South German Pilsner); *Sauerländer Pilstypus* (Sauerland Pilsner-type); and *hanseatische Pilsnertyp* (Hanseatic Pilsner-type). It is the only style that is brewed in every German *land* (state).

Klassische Pilsner has more stress placed on the hops. It is precisely crafted to be robust, have a full mouth-feel, and be well-rounded.

Süddeutschen Pilsner is more robust and has more aromatic malt aroma than the German norm for the style.

Sauerländer Pilstypus is particularly light and delicate, but not very bitter at all. It is, often enough, easily identified because of its particularly light color.

Hanseatische Pilsnertyp is particularly bitter, dry and sharp-tasting from the hops. This North German style is mostly found around Jever.

If there were a 'standard' German Pils, the profile might read:

Color 3–4SRM, 7–10EBC; bitterness 30–40IBUS; alcohol content 1044–50, 4.0–5.0% ABV.

Pilsner, Pilsner, Pils–Bohemia–Czech Republic

These are similar to German Pils, but are fuller in body, and may have a little more color. The head should be white and dense, and there should be a delightful balance between hop and malt. The body should be medium, and malt should be apparent in the palate. The finish should be clean and of moderate duration. Bohemia, in the Czech Republic, is where the Pils style originated.

Compared to Export Lager, Pils is a little less alcoholic, but much more finely hopped. It is a bit slimmer or more delicate in taste, and has a brighter mouthfeel.

Color 3–5SRM, 7–14EBC; bitterness 35–45IBUS; alcohol content 1044–56OG, 4.0–5.0% ABV.

Diät Pils–Germany

This is an odd style, deserving its own classification. Little-known in North America, German brewers developed it as a beer for diabetics. It is very low in carbohydrates because it is fully attenuated. However, because full attenuation elevates alcohol content, it is full of calories, so it should not be confused with Light (low-caloric) Lager regardless what the name might suggest.

It has plenty of hop notes, both in the aroma and on the palate. Alcohol content 5.8% ABV.

Dortmunder-Export–Germany

Export originated in Dortmund, and has now spread throughout most of Germany. Only beer brewed in Dortmund itself can be labelled Dortmunder. Others, brewed outside the city, are labelled 'Export' or 'Dortmund-style'. Unfortunately, this style has a blue-collar image in the Dortmund district, as Export is a favorite of the workers in this industrial area. The brewers, ever-conscious of their image, do very little to promote it, preferring instead to concentrate on Pilsners. However, for years brewers elsewhere, especially in Belgium and the Netherlands, have produced this style. Many breweries founded by German immigrants in North America also brewed it.

Export has a bigger body than Pilsners, and is not as hoppy/dry. Nor is it as sweet as Münchener Lager, so the style falls between the other two, but Export is stronger than both. In other countries, brewers use the term Export to indicate a premium beer. Alcohol content is 5.25–5.5% ABV.

As is often the case in Germany, different regions brew their beers to slightly different specifications. German Export is light-golden to deep golden in color, with a full mouth-feel. The South German type has a malt-dominant aroma. The North German type is the opposite–the aroma is hops-dominant. Do you notice the trend here? North Germans prefer much more hops in their beers than do South Germans, who prefer malt over hops. This applies to both aroma and palate. Bitterness, too, is between that of Pilsners and Müncheners. Hops used are Hallertauer, Northern Brewer, Spalt or Tettnang.

Color 4–6SRM, 9–15EBC; bitterness 24–37IBUS; alcohol content 1048–560G, 4.8–6.0% ABV.

Münchener (Munich) Bayerisches Helles–Germany

The style is alternately called Munich or Bavarian since it has now spread throughout that southern German region. Munich is the capitol of that state.

It is the maltiest of the four major German lager styles. Mouth-feel is modest, hop aroma is mild, and it is mostly malt in the aroma.

Hell, the German word for light (colored), is the every-day Bavarian session beer. The color is golden; alcohol content moderate; bitterness is nicely balanced by malt sweetness. Carbonation is average. Helles doesn't reach as high up the alcohol content scale as do Dunkles, but the other parameters are about the same. This style developed in the early 20th century. Prior to then, Bavarian brewers mostly produced dark beers, but they noticed the popularity of pale beers brewed elsewhere in Germany and the rest of Europe and started brewing it themselves. Little could they know how popular it would become.

Color 3–5srm, 7–14ebc; bitterness 18–25ibus; alcohol content 1046–550g, 4.5–5.5% abv.

Bière de Paris–France

These are similar in style to *Bière de gardes,* but are not. Close, but no bière. They are distinctly Parisienne. Like *Bières de garde,* they come in wine bottles, but they are lagers instead of ales. Parallel to the development of bottom-fermenting yeast in the caves of Bayern, a similar activity was occurring in the Paris region. A distinct lager yeast strain developed.

The style, previously, was known as *brune de Paris* (Paris Brown) is unique to Paris and environs. The beers were strong and amber-colored. That tradition continues.

People think of France as a nation of wine-drinkers. Whilst true, the history of brewing in Paris dates to Roman times. At the time of their Revolution, there were 28 breweries in the city. They were established in a section called *La Glacière* (The Ice-house).

Bière de Garde Lager–France

This style split from its ale version when some brewers took to using bottom-fermenting lager yeast instead of traditional ale yeast. Though not as common as the original, interest in, and the availability of, beers brewed in the north of France continues to increase. Normally, these beers are not pasteurized, and are in the 76cl champagne-style, corked bottles with the wired down caps. They are matured for three months.

Color ranges from blonde to brown. Alcohol warming should be noticeable, and the body should be medium.

Color 4–14SRM, 7–35EBC; bitterness 25–35IBUS; alcohol content 1050–800G, 5.0–8.0% ABV.

Märzenbier–Germany

This style is very similar to the Wiener (Vienna) style, but it is not the same. Some lump them, and Festbiers, together. I do not. It is the third classic German beer style.

Märzen was developed before the advance of refrigeration. Each March *(März* is March, the month, in German) brewers would brew an extra-strong beer to survive the long warm months of summer, until it was unveiled at the end of that season. Its last stocks were finished in October. It was brewed as the last batch of the winter brewing season (this, before modern refrigeration made it possible to brew year-round).

Color is deep golden or a rich saturated yellow to pretty copper, which is most-common. Märzen is malty, both in nose and palate. Mouthfeel is full, and alcohol content is moderate, and in decline.

Color 4–15SRM, 10–35EBC; bitterness 18–25IBUS; alcohol content 1050–560G, 4.8–5.9% ABV.

Wiener (Viennese)–Austria

This is the fourth of the classic German Lager styles, though its brewing has died out in Wien (Vienna). The city, though, is still honoured by the use of its name in the English-speaking world.

Wienerbier is a close cousin of Märzen, but is a little stronger than its German relative. This style developed in Wien, Austria. Strangely, this is a style hardly brewed there any longer. Stranger still, Mexico is the largest producer of this beer, and it is frequently brewed throughout Central and South Americas.

The style features medium-strong alcohol content. Color range is amber-red or copper to medium brown. Bitterness is moderate. Hoppiness in the aroma is light, and the palate is malty.

It is important to note that nowhere in our German references are any of the four classic German styles, except Pilsners, referred to by their city's names. We English-speakers are the ones who gave them city names.

Color 8–12SRM, 16–30EBC; bitterness 22–35IBUS; alcohol content 1048–600G, 4.8–6.0% ABV.

Amber Lager–North America craft

This newly developing style, which includes 'Red Lager', seems to be a rejuvenation of the above-mentioned Wiener style, but made with North American-grown ingredients.

Color is amber, red, or copper. Body is medium. A certain caramel malt character is often evident in the aroma, and on the palate. Hop notes range from low to very high, again in both the aroma and on the palate.

Color 6–12SRM, 15–30EBC; bitterness 20–30IBUS; alcohol content 1042–560G, 4.8–5.4% ABV.

Dark lagers

Dark Lager–North America

This not-so-dark Lager is virtually the same as its Light counter-part–except for color. Some are simply darkened by with caramel syrup. Some might be darkened with a pinch of Münchener or black malt. The color is not nearly as dark as German Dunkles.

Hop and malt taste in these beers is minimal, as is hop character, aroma and bouquet. Body is light. Carbonation is rather high, and similar to Standard Lager.

Color 10–20SRM, 20–80EBC; bitterness 9–15IBUS; alcohol content 1040–480G, 4.0–5.0% ABV.

Oud Bruin (Old Brown)–The Netherlands

Not to be confused with the Belgian Ale with the same name, this Lager is from the Netherlands. It is a low-alcohol beer with a 2.0–3.5% ABV. At its upper end, the alcohol content is comparable with English Mild. It is a very sweet beer, and is classified in the Netherlands as a *Tafelbier* (Table beer). This is not a style one would make a special trip to the Netherlands to seek.

Some experts classify Oud Bruin all by itself in a style named Weak Lager. It seems a bit much to give a solitary beer its own category unless it is so singular that it fits nowhere else. This doesn't.

Dunkles (dark)–Germany

Breweries in the north and west of Germany don't usually have *Dunklesbier* in their assortment. It is a style of Munich and Bavaria. Like schwarzbier, it is popular with students, but doesn't have a large following in the general public.

Color is dark-amber to dark brown. Carbonation is average or normal. Aroma has pronounced chocolate, roasted malt, and bread notes. The taste can best be described as malty, with only clean, mild, hop bitterness. The body is medium.

Color 17–20SRM, 40–80EBC; bitterness 20–45IBUS; alcohol content 1048–1063OG, 4.8–6.3% ABV.

Schwarzbier (black beer)–Germany

It is alternatively called *Schwarzes Pils* (Black Pils) or *Schwarzbier* (Black Beer).

This style should have soft roast malt notes in the nose. The body is full to very full. Hop aromas should be noticeable, pleasant, but low. Hop and roasted malt bitterness in the palate should be low to medium.

Color 25–30SRM, 100–120EBC; bitterness 20–32IBUS; alcohol content 1044–56OG, 5.0–5.5% ABV.

Bock Beers

All Bock beer is in the German *Starkbier* (strong beer) class. The *Starkbier* class encompasses all lagers between 6.25–12.5% ABV; >1064OG. There are several Bockbier styles (See below for the others.)

Germans describe *Bockbier* as being light- or dark-colored; filtered or with active yeast; little hop bitterness; very full-mouthed; and with strong to very strong malt in the palate.

Bockbier was first brewed in Einbeck, a Hanseatic city in Niedersachsen (Lower Saxony). Therefore, a Bockbier from there, Einbecker Ur-Bock, gets to carry the "Ur" (Original) in its name.

The town has a very long brewing history and rivalry with München. Martin Luther fortified himself during the Diet of Worms in the 1500s with bockbier from Einbeck. München has tried to lay claim to Bockbier as one of their own styles ever since a North German duke married a southern noble woman. He brought with him several *Fäßer* (barrels) of Bockbier. Evidently it was a smashing success. Einbeck's height of brewing was in the 1600s. It seems the whole town consisted of brewers—about 700 of them. The Braumeister would take some of his apprentices or workers and go with the city-owned brew kettle house to house so each could brew their own beer. How's that for municipal services?

Einbeck, being a Hanseatic trading city, brewed its beers strong to survive long journeys, much in the same way that traditional IPAs developed. It is believed that the first *Bockbiere* were top-fermented wheat beers of dark color. Since the development of lager yeast, they are bottom-fermented and have developed into Helles and Dunkles styles.

Doppelbocks (Double Bocks)—Germany

These are the stronger brothers of Bocks. Alcohol content is 7.2–7.5 ABV, >1074OG. Bitterness range is 25–40IBUs, but is overpowered by the malt. Color can be Helles or Dunkles; very full-mouthed; it has a pronounced malt aroma. Grains used in Doppelbocks are pale Munich, dark Munich, black malt, carapils and dextrin. Hallertauer hops are used. Too, Doppelbocks may be considered the lager equivalent of Barleywine.

Doppelbocks can, quite often, be distinguished from Bocks by their label because the brand names usually end in *ator*, Doppelbock's traditional designator.

Color 12–30SRM, 30–120EBC; bitterness 17–27IBUs; alcohol content 1074–80OG, 6.5–8.0% ABV.

Eisbock–Germany

Eis in German means ice. What does ice have to do with beer? In this instance, water is removed from the beer by freezing it. Water has a higher freezing point than does alcohol. The beer is cooled until the water freezes. At that point, as ice, it is separated from the beer. What remains is a very sweet-tasting beer with a higher alcohol content, and a very malty aroma. The main reason it is so sweet is that it is not balanced by bittering hops.

Color 18–50SRM, 42–200EBC; bitterness 26–33IBUs; alcohol content 1092–1116OG, 8.6–14.8% ABV.

Maibock–Germany

This style is a super-premium Bock made for spring celebrations such as Maypole Day. They are released each year on May 1.

There's malt in the nose and the palate. Body is medium to full, and the finish is long-lasting. Malt should predominate. Hops should be noticeable, but low to medium.

Color 4–10SRM, 10–20EBC; bitterness 20–25IBUs; alcohol content 1066–68OG; 6.5–7.0% ABV.

Meibok–The Netherlands

The Dutch version of the German style. Color range is narrow, from amber to copper. Alcohol strength is stronger (7.0–7.5% ABV) than is common Bock. Meiboks are sweeter with a more substantial character than the Bokbiers of early autumn. They also have a stronger finish. Some lump Meiboks with common Bokbiers, but the two styles are dissimilar enough to separate them.

About half the Meiboks produced are Ale Boks (top-fermented). Each has its own style, and therefore its own listing.

Bokbier–The Netherlands

This is a Bockbier derivative brewed in The Netherlands. It is different than the German version, so it warrants spelling *Bock* in Dutch, and giving it its own style.

It has been mooted that the style brewed in the Netherlands is merely an adaptation of the German. However, beer historians in the former country claim their style has existed "since before the birth of Moses". Whilst that might be stretching things a bit, farmers there have been brewing strong dark beers there for centuries. Furthermore, unlike German Bockbier, which took its corrupted name from Einbeck, the city where it was first brewed, the Netherlands' style was named *Bok*, 'goat' in English because it kicks like one.

In The Netherlands, the style developed originally as a dark beer, which was brewed once a year in June. It was released in October, and was available just in that month.

By 1970 the style had died out in The Netherlands, but beer drinkers took up its cause and it was re-introduced. By 1991 about 30 different brands were brewed. A few Dutch brewers are breaking away from the June-only brewing, and are now producing it year round. The styles main differences to the German Bockbier is that the Dutch version is hopped to a greater extent, and is dryer, which is apparent in the palate, and they tend to be brown, though some are the color of Pale Ale.

The alcohol content of Bokbier is 6.5–7.0% ABV.

Dubbelbok–The Netherlands

The Doppelbock style has not yet fully developed in the Netherlands. We'll give it its own style listing here, and watch if it fills up.

Brand also has an ABV 7.5% Dubbelbok, simply called Brand Duppelbock (some brewers maintain the German spelling).

More than ten Dutch, and several Belgian brewers have taken to brewing Ale Boks, which are not to be confused with these Lagers.

Bock—North America craft

This is a style I am waiting to develop. There are a few from brew-pubs and microbreweries producing it, but none with wide-spread distribution.

I suggest this category should be very close to, if not matching, German parameters, with the difference being the use of North American-grown grains and hops. For a beer to qualify for this category, it should meet these criteria.

Double Bock—North America craft

The new brewers are starting to turn out some excellent Double Bocks, though they may not all adhere to German brewing specifications, most notably in alcohol content. Some have gained regional and even national availability. This is a good sign.

Bock & Double Bock—North America

Like many North American styles, this style bock seldom measures up to its European counterpart. There are exceptions.

In Germany the dividing line between regular Lager and Bock is alcohol content. Beer must be at least 1064OG, 6.4% ABV to be classified as Bockbier. In North America, Bock has 4.5–5.0% ABV. They are often Standard Lagers with caramel syrup added to darken them. However, some are legitimately brewed using dark malts. Carbonation tends to be moderate.

North American Bocks were first developed round the mid-1800s. Then, they were a seasonal beer, brewed and lagered through the winter, and released in the spring, as was Germanic practice. As with many things relating to beer, Prohibition killed Bock. It enjoyed a brief spurt when Prohibition was repealed (December 1933), but not long afterwards production stopped due to declining sales. It was revived in the 1970s by a few brewers, but has languished until recently.

Strong Pils–Europe

This classification is for Pilsners brewed with ≥7.0% ABV. In Germany, the Bock style parameters kick in at ≥ 6.5% ABV, so this style is analogous with a blond Bock.

Color is about the same as standard Euro-Pils. The body is medium, with noticeable alcoholic warming. There is no mistaking the strength of these beers.

Rauchbier–Germany

This is a style from Bamberg in Franconia, a district in Northern Bavaria. The name means Smoked Beer. The malts are dried over beech chips. During the process the smoke penetrates the malt, which then passes the flavor and odor to the beer during the brewing process. Alcohol content is moderate. Color range is medium brown to very dark. The smoked aroma is fine to very strong. Malt is still apparent in the aroma. Hop bitterness runs from delicate to robust. Mostly brands are lagered in barrels in the traditional manner.

Color 10–20SRM, 20–80EBC; bitterness 20–30IBUS; alcohol content 1048–520G, 4.3–5.0 ABV.

Lager-Ale Hybrids

LAGER-ALE HYBRIDS are beers brewed with lager yeast strains, but fermented at ale (warm) temperatures, before being cold-aged as are lagers. They are the opposites of Ale-Lager hybrids. These beers often develop out of habit or necessity.

Bok Ales—The Netherlands

Like their Pils Ale, the Dutch have taken to brewing Bok Ale, another hybrid. Unlike their lager cousins, German Bock and Maibock, Bok Ale is top-fermented. It cannot be compared directly with Bocks (which are lagers) nor with Brown Ales (regular or strong).

Malt Liquors—North America

Here is another hybrid, a lager fermented at ale temperatures, then lagered at 32–35°F for one to five weeks.

It is best drunk ice-cold (32–35°F).

This style is diverse. Alcohol content mary vary from just above Premium Lager beer strength to German Dopplebock levels. There is no hop nose. The high alcohol content is often the result of adding dextrose (corn sugar or syrup) Bitterness is non-existent, hopping rates being sub-threshold. The low OG is the absolute minimum allowable under law for it to be called a malt-beverage. Residual malt sweetness might be perceived. Then again, it might not.

Contents: 50–60% barley malt, 30–40% corn grits, 10–20% dextrose.

Color 2–5SRM, 4–8EBC; bitterness 5–14IBUS; alcohol content 1050–800G, 6.25–8.1% ABV.

California Common Beer–North America craft

This is the one true American-developed beer style still being brewed. It's more-common name is Steam Beer, but as Anchor Brewing, of San Francisco, California has trademarked that name, an alternative had to be invented, hence the California Common Beer moniker. It was first brewed during the Gold Rush era (late 1800s) in the San Francisco bay area. The style spread all across the West Coast, to Alaska, Idaho, and as far east as Wisconsin.

Since I use yeast-type as the determining factor of classification, California Common Beer is placed with Lagers.

Wide, shallow fermenting vessels are used, similar to some British and European fermenters, but quite in contrast with today's vertical cylindrical-conical vessels.

The color range of original California Common Beer was all over the place–light to dark. Now it seems to have settled on amber. They are medium in alcoholic strength. In addition, they are hoppy beers, both in aroma and in taste.

Color 10–20SRM; bitterness 30–45IBUS; alcohol content 1044–560G, 4.4–5.6% ABV.

Kentucky Common Beer (extinct)–United States

This eponymous beer was quite popular round the turn of this century. Similar in nature to California Common Beer, the Kentucky style had about the same starting gravity, but was less-attenuated. The result was a beer with less alcohol. Bittering was less than its flourishing California cousin.

Sadly, this style died out, replaced in favor by Standard Lager. However, with the establishment of micro-breweries and brew-pubs in Kentucky, there is hope some might re-introduce the style.

Some research has been done on the style by local home-brewers, who are often at the forefront of style rebirths.

Color: not available; bitterness about 27IBUs; alcohol content 1045–500G, 3.8–4.5% ABV.

Stout Lager

This is another new style, a bottom-fermented Stout of medium-strong alcohol content. The stronger style dark beers are re-appearing as public interest returned after many year's absence. There are only a few brands in this style at the moment, but this situation should change for the better.

Many traditional top-fermented Stouts now have lower alcohol contents than these Lager Stouts.

Porter Lager–Denmark

This style is brewed in Denmark and elsewhere in northern Europe. It is a Porter brewed with lager yeast, but fermented at ale temperatures. The style simply came about because brewers chose to use lager yeast, which was customary in their countries, to ale yeasts, which were not. The oldest brewery in the States also brews a Porter Lager. The style closely resembles a Bavarian Dunkel in character.

Other lagers

Winter Lagers/Festbier

This is not so much a style as another catch-all group because the range of beers in it is too broad to define. It is similar to the Grand Cru group of beers, in that any beer a brewer designates as "Christmas", "Festival", "Winter Holidays", "Harvest" beer would fall into this group.

Generally speaking, these beers have a higher alcohol content than the brewer's standard offerings. As with the matching ales group, alcohol content should be above 6.5% ABV to make the beers substantially different and notable. In addition, spices, herbs, and other such ingredients may be used to add something special to it. They are, also, not available year-round.

Lager Wheat–North America craft

This is a newly emerging style. Its was developed by brew-pubs and micro-brewers, and is similar to the North American Wheat Ale, except that lager, rather than ale yeast is used.

Wheat content should be 30–50%. Compared with German Weizenbier, this style shows none of the phenolic clove notes. Fruity, estery notes in both the nose and palate are typical. It also has higher hops rates, but lower carbonation than the German styles. Alcohol content is moderate.

Color is most-typically golden to light amber. Body should be light to medium. There should be no buttery or butterscotch notes on the palate.

Color 2–8SRM, 4–16EBC; bitterness 10–20IBUS; alcohol content 1040–500G, 4.0–5.0% ABV.